WORLD WAR II FROM ORIGINAL SOURCES

TACTICS OF THE IMPERIAL JAPANESE ARMY

BOB CARRUTHERS

This book is published in Great Britain in 2013 by
Coda Books Ltd,Office Suite 2, Shrieves Walk, Sheep Street, Stratford upon Avon, Warwickshire CV37 6GJ.
www.codabooks.com

ISBN 978-1-78158-324-1

A CIP catalogue record for this book is available from the British Library.

CONTENTS

INTRODUCTION

The attack on Pearl Harbour on 7th December 1941 finally decided the long debated question as to whether or not the USA would enter the Second World War. While the US was busy assembling its new armies, navies and air forces the US Intelligence Service was already beginning to collate intelligence on its new Japanese enemy. This information was organised and disseminated to the troops who needed it, in the form of two main monthly intelligence bulletins. These were *Tactical and Technical Trends* which first appeared in June 1942 and the *Intelligence Bulletin* which began to appear from September 1942 onwards. All of the articles collected together here are taken from *Tactical and Technical Trends* and appeared from 1942 to late 1944.

The main focus for the US was initially on the war with Japan and a great majority of the early reports which were published in *Tactical and Technical Trends* are concerned with the war in the Pacific. However, as America began to get to grips with the notion that the country was now at war, British and Commonwealth forces were already heavily engaged with the Japanese in Burma, Malaya, New Guinea, Indonesia and elsewhere. The vast majority of those early reports concerned the fighting conducted by the British forces and it is those reports which form the bulk of what you are about to read here.

The material for the two US intelligence journals was originally collected from British combat reports, captured Japanese documents, P.O.W debriefs and Japanese training manuals. As such the quality of much of what was printed was highly variable, some reports are highly accurate while, in others, the precision of the information is questionable to say the least, but that's what makes these reports so fascinating. Regardless of the overall accuracy this is a priceless glimpse into how the men in the front lines learned about their enemy, and as such it presents us with an invaluable insight into the events of the war with Japan were perceived at the time when they actually unfolded. The reports also provide us with a host of information concerning the minor aspects of the thousands of tactical combats being waged day in and day out which expand our knowledge of the realities of the fighting in World War II.

Thank you for buying this book. I hope you enjoy reading these long forgotten reports as much as I enjoyed discovering them and collating them for you. Other volumes in this series are already in preparation and I hope you will decide to join me in other discoveries as the series develops.

Bob Carruthers
Berchtesgaden 2013

ORGANIZATION OF JAP ANTI-TANK COMPANY

Tactical and Technical Trends, No. 1, June 18, 1942.

Following is the composition of a Japanese Independent Anti-Tank Company operating in Burma:

ORGANIZATION

The total strength of the company is approximately 150.

EQUIPMENT

Eight 37 mm Anti-tank guns. Each gun is carried on a 1 1/2 ton truck. 150 rounds of ammunition are carried in each truck. No motor transport is provided for the men.

TACTICAL EMPLOYMENT

The unit was subdivided in the advance on Rangoon. Two platoons were with the 33rd Division and two with the 55th Division. The two platoons with the 55th Division were to operate with Japanese tanks, but failed to do so because the tanks could not cross the Sittang River in time.

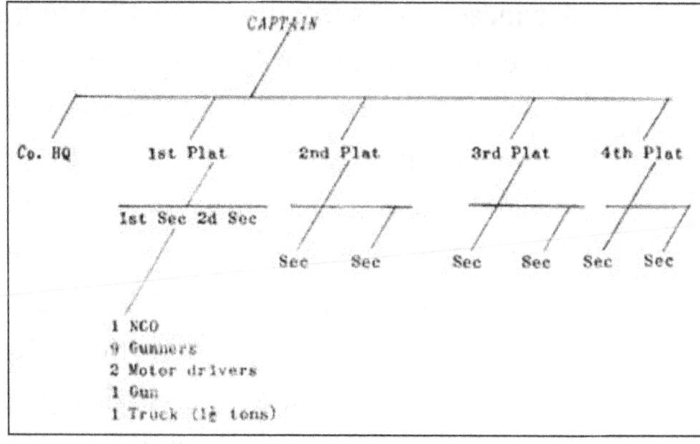

JAPANESE TACTICS IN THE PHILIPPINES

Tactical and Technical Trends, No. 6, August 27, 1942.

The following comments and lessons on Japanese tactics and equipment have been gathered in interviews with officers who served with Filipino and American troops during the campaign in Luzon. They do not represent a complete survey of Japanese tactics and equipment, but are rather the 'observations of individual officers on what they saw and what impressed them.

The Japanese soldiers were fairly young, their average age being about 22 to 23, although the best troops were about 25, many of whom had had experience in China.

The Japanese have troops trained primarily for beach landing. Specially built barges drawn by motor boats carry 80 or more men. Landings were usually made at night; when possible, during a full moon. Ordinarily, the landings were made about midnight, with the barges coming as far in on the beach as possible.

Although the Japanese have specially trained landing troops they did not always employ them, particularly when they knew the opposition would not be strong. Whenever the Japanese did encounter strong resistance in an attempted landing, they simply moved to another location and landed where the enemy was not present. After landing, they would attempt to push inland and encircle the troops along the shore.

No Japanese parachute troops were employed in the Philippines. The Japanese did, however, utilize parachutes in dropping bales of propaganda and in dropping food and ammunition to troops who had been isolated from their main forces.

As in every other campaign in the Far East, the principal tactics used by the Japanese centered on their ability to infiltrate. The actual infiltrations were usually carried out at night. The Japanese would work their way forward in small parties through gaps, around flanks, and even through the front lines. They would remain quiet during the following day, and on the next night more troops would infiltrate the American position until there was a sufficiently strong force actually in or behind the American lines to launch a small attack. In these infiltration tactics the Japanese were capitalizing on the initiative and "fanaticism" of the individual soldier.

American officers seem to agree that this "fanaticism" manifests itself particularly in lack of fear of death. As one officer puts it, "they will do things that they know will cost them their lives; for example, throw themselves on wire so that the following troops may pass over their bodies, or destroy tank mines by deliberately walking on them." In actual battle they are ferocious fighters. They very rarely surrender, because they fear what their captors will do to them and because they believe that if they die they go to Heaven and their families are honored. They also believe that if they surrender and are later retaken by their own troops, their families will be disgraced and they themselves will be punished. Even when surrounded, individual groups and soldiers will continue to fight on. One occasion has been reported when U.S. forces surrounded about 2,000 Japanese behind the American lines; about 200 got away, but the rest fought so savagely, refusing to surrender, that only about 50 were left to be captured. Many Japanese will even go so far as to commit suicide rather than be taken prisoner.

Another instance of the excellent fighting qualities of the individual Japanese soldier was illustrated in the extensive use of snipers. Apparently the members of the sniper corps were a picked group, for their marksmanship was extremely good, and they had been provided with special clothing. The footwear of the sniper was a split-toe, rubber-soled sneaker with a cloth top. He wore a head net over a steel helmet; and a loose shirt or smock of green and white replaced the usual uniform. Green sprigs and leaves were inserted in the head net over his helmet. Climbing a tree, the sniper would hide in the foliage after tying himself to the tree with vines or rope. There he would wait patiently for a suitable target. These snipers apparently had instructions to concentrate on the American officers, for often they would let a whole detachment of Filipino or American enlisted men go by in order to wait for a shot at an officer. The snipers employed the regular .25 caliber rifle of the ground troops, using powder which gave no flash, no smoke, and "a report not much louder than that of a B-B gun."

Characteristic of Japanese tactics was the attack at dusk. Infiltrating and moving around to the flanks, they would take as much territory as possible before actual darkness fell. During the night, positions would be consolidated so that by dawn they would have their recently occupied ground well organized against possible U.S. counterattacks. At all times the Japanese kept up a pressure against our lines, constantly seeking gaps and weak spots. When one was found, a small group would go in as far as possible, to be followed by more unless the first, were immediately wiped out.

The Japanese had a novel method of serving their light machine gun. One man served as the mount, the second man was gunner. They would both drop to the ground and as soon as they had finished a clip, they would roll over, crawl away about 10 or more yards and then open up on the same targets. This had the effect of confusing the American and Filipino troops as to the exact position of the enemy, sometimes leading them to believe that there were two or more machine guns operating against them. The gun used was not a tommy gun, as many thought, but simply the Nambu light .25 caliber machine gun.

The Japanese artillery employed a fifth gun in many batteries. While the battery was firing, the fifth gun would range and obtain data for new targets, and after the four guns of the firing battery had accomplished their first mission they could then shift to the new target without delay. The Japanese handled their artillery well, except that in the beginning of the campaign their disposition of guns and batteries showed that they had not had much experience against an enemy who also used artillery. For example, initially there was very little attempt to conceal or camouflage the Japanese guns. After their artillery had been subjected to severe concentrations by the U.S. artillery, however, they learned quickly. Another mistake made at first was bringing up truck columns under U.S. artillery fire or attempting to occupy towns which were well within our artillery range, but the heavy casualties suffered soon taught them the value of camouflage and dispersion. The Japanese artillery fire was ordinarily accurate. They used the 105-mm. and 150-mm. guns, both of which were excellent. The range of the 105 is approximately 20,000 yards, that of the 150, 27,000 yards. The few 240-mm. pieces were not extensively used.

At first Japanese counterbattery fire was not good. There were probably two reasons for this: first, as already stated, the Japanese had never before been up against an enemy who had much artillery, that is, enough to make real counterbattery worth while; second, the U.S. counterbattery fire was so excellent that it more or less neutralized the Japanese artillery. At the end, however, when they were bombarding Corregidor, their counterbattery fire was very good.

Another characteristic of the Japanese was the apparent importance they attached to harassing tactics, with the object of creating confusion and indecision in the minds of their enemy.

In these operations, which they kept up constantly, they utilized individuals and small groups to fire from unexpected positions, conduct sniping operations, and demonstrate in unexpected places. As reported in the newspapers, they would often use firecrackers to achieve this confusion. Bunches of firecrackers were set off at different positions in front of the U.S. lines, on their flanks, and even behind the lines. In so doing, they hoped to confuse U.S. troops as to the actual Japanese position, and also to draw U.S. fire and thus locate machine-gun and rifle groups. These tactics were effective against raw troops, but their effect decreased soon after soldiers had been exposed to them.

The Japanese had almost complete control of the air, and they utilized it to observe, bomb, and strafe the U.S. and Filipino troops. Most of the bombing was high-level; dive bombing was used occasionally but only against front-line troops. Against rear-area installations high-level attacks were always used. Ordinarily these high-level attacks were kept up to about 20,000 or 30,000 feet by U.S. antiaircraft.

Reports varied on the effectiveness of the Japanese Fifth Column activity. Apparently the Japanese attempted to use Fifth Column rather extensive but had only fair results. Some fires were lit on the beaches and in jungles, and some signals given with flares and flashlights. Many of the flares were lighted by the Japanese themselves with the object of creating confusion among the U.S. troops.

The Japanese also used propaganda directed against both the Army and the civilians. How effective it was is not yet known, but the significant thing is that they did seriously try to use it, and may be expected to use it every time they feel there is any chance of obtaining results.

From Japanese activities in the Philippine campaign it is apparent that they will attempt, whenever possible, to tap wires and intercept radio messages. U.S. officers who fought in the

Philippines emphasize that all conversations should be in code. There should be no reference to numerical designations or to individuals.

The Japanese also attempted to capitalize on the large number of refugees, driving them into the U.S. lines, thus adding to our burden of supply. It is reported that between 10,000 and 30,000 refugees flooded Bataan.

One officer gives the following comment as the most important generalization to be made on the Japanese soldier: "The Japanese are crafty, shrewd, given to deception. They are amazingly patient and wait hours, even days, for their chance. They are tough individual soldiers and work well in small groups of two or three men."

Another officer gives the following observation: "Don't underestimate the Jap. He is patient, an individualist, taught to go by himself. He does not fear capture when he gets behind your line. Guard your headquarters. He works at night. He is full of trickery; he knows English, will learn your name, call to you, get you off your guard, and kill you. He is a past master at using devices to annoy you and work on your morale even though these devices may have little other material effect. He doesn't surrender and in battle is a savage fighter."

JAPANESE TACTICS IN BURMA

Tactical and Technical Trends, No. 7, September 10, 1942.

The following information is based on a report by a British officer of the fighting in Burma. As will be readily seen it is not a complete analysis, but simply a collection of miscellaneous notes.

Tactically the Japanese relied for the most part on the ambush. The ambushes were generally very skillfully located, but were always on the same pattern, particularly with reference to the positions of weapons.

The chief form of enemy defense encountered was a combination road-block and ambush. The position was invariably located at a point where woods converged on the road. Covering weapons were effectively located. Light machine guns in dispersed positions were placed forward of the woods, and snipers spotted in the woods to prevent envelopment of the position. The road-block is also covered by one or more heavy weapons. In three instances a French 75 (probably taken in Indo-China) was encountered at a road-block. In each instance the block was in a bend of the road, and the gun was placed in a concealed position off the road about 50 yards beyond the block on a line in prolongation of the original direction of the road. To knock out this gun the area may be searched with artillery and mortar fire, but its elimination is primarily an infantry task to be accomplished by mopping up the gun crew with small arms. In addition, a 37-mm antitank gun may be placed very close to the road-block, usually on the opposite side of the road to the 75-mm gun; a 4-inch mortar may be emplaced further to the rear.

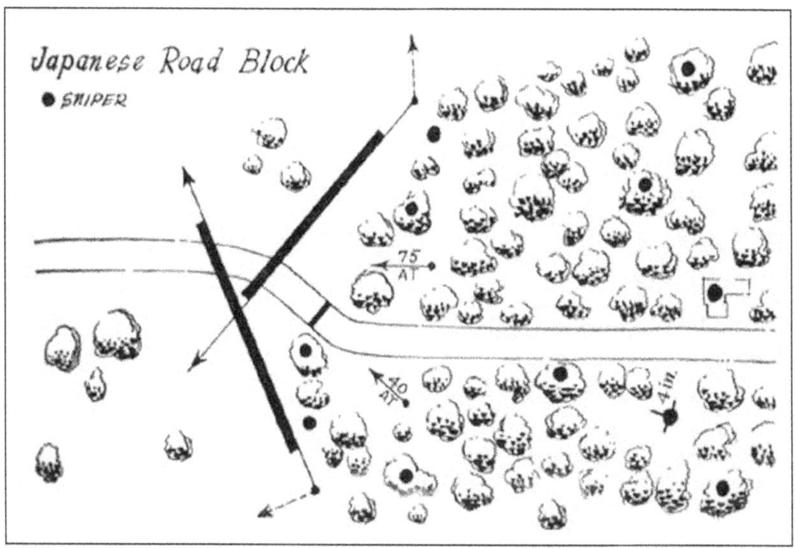

The Japanese 37-mm antitank gun is only 2 feet high, being supported on small wheels. It is thus easily concealed and is usually put in position in a ditch or in the shadow of a building. It may also be found near culverts which the crews use when being shelled.

The Japanese 4-inch mortar is not as highly effective as some reports would indicate. For effect it depends entirely upon blast and its killing power is very limited. One of its chief dangers is its incendiary powers against halted vehicles. When attacked by British mortar fire, the fire of this weapon became inaccurate. If the counter-mortar fire was at all accurate the enemy moved the gun. As soon as its position has been determined, it should be overrun by infantry. When the 4-inch mortar is used in support of road blocks it is generally emplaced near the road, but farther to the rear than the 75-mm and antitank guns.

The Japanese have invariably emplaced their light machine guns a short distance in front of the forward edge of a woods. This is done in order to escape artillery or mortar fire which may be directed at the edge of the woods. The machine guns are not dug in, but they are cleverly concealed by use of background;

every precaution is taken to eliminate splash. The guns are normally fired on fixed lines along the edge of the woods. In attacking the machine guns, artillery and mortar fire should start some 50 yards in front of the edge of the woods, and the leading infantry must follow the barrage as closely as possible. Any formation in line, or bunching, by the attacking infantry is suicidal. From the jump-off point until the objective is overrun the infantry must remain widely dispersed; within platoons at least one section should be held in reserve, and sections should maintain a patrol formation.

In wood and jungle fighting the Japanese snipers presented a most difficult problem. They remained at their posts with great bravery, and in the opinion of the reporting officer they had been assigned a definite time to remain there. Snipers took positions in trees, on the ground, and in houses. The elimination of snipers in trees or on the ground is the task of the individual soldier. Care must be taken not to advance in a straight line; one should get behind a tree, observe in all directions, both on the ground and up in the tree, and then move very rapidly to a tree about 10 yards to the right or left front. This process is repeated, and it is probable that the sniper will either be spotted or that the stalker will get behind him, and have the sniper at his mercy. Snipers posted in houses present a different problem, and experience shows that too many casualties occur if stalking is attempted. The best means of attack appears to be either to burn them out or use grenades under the protection of smoke.

The Japanese were very adept in the use of camouflage and altered their appearance according to the nature of the terrain that they were traversing. Examples of their use of camouflage were these: a green net for the helmet, long green gloves, bottle-green liquid carried to color face and rifle, different colored shirts carried by the individual soldier, and elephants colored with varying shades of green paint.

NOTES ON THE BURMA CAMPAIGN

Tactical and Technical Trends, No. 9, October 8, 1942.

The following observations are taken from British sources which summarize the experience gained from the campaign in Burma. The lessons drawn from this campaign must be viewed in the light of the conditions under which the fighting took place: outnumbered United Nations forces were conducting a very difficult retreat, in country which was mainly jungle and where many natives were Fifth Columnists.

A. TRAINING FOR JUNGLE WARFARE

The British report emphasizes that, for troops unfamiliar with the jungle, first contact with this type of country is confusing and even frightening. The Japanese capitalized on this by the use of fire-crackers and "battle cries" to add to the effect of jungle noises. Troops who are to operate in jungle country should be trained as far as possible under conditions which will familiarize them with this type of terrain.

The report recommends that troops be trained in the use of battle cries, both for purposes of controlling movement and for the psychological effect on enemy morale. The Japanese have made effective use of this device.

B. MOVEMENT

The Japanese made little or no use of scouts during night movements, and in some cases they advanced without putting out patrols ahead of their columns. The Japanese were also careless in moving motor transport and normally gave their approach away by failing to dim the headlights.

In the second half of the campaign, the Japanese moved by night and rested during the day. During this period, they made very inadequate provision for security of their bivouacs and were easily surprised during daylight.

C. FIFTH COLUMNISTS

These were used extensively, sometimes as patrols moving ahead of advancing Japanese forces and sending back information. British ambushes were nearly always given away to the enemy by Fifth Columnists.

D. JAPANESE SHOCK TROOPS

These are killers, trained in individual fighting, self-reliant, and bold to the point of fanaticism. Moreover, they have a very good sense of guerrilla tactics and are capable of effective action in groups. They are masters of the art of concealment and camouflage, and very quick to size up a tactical situation.

Usually armed with light automatic weapons, their sniping has sometimes been deadly, but it is reported that, on the whole, their marksmanship is not adequate to enable them to reap the full benefits of their excellent offensive tactics.

The shock troops are employed primarily for infiltration. They sift through forward lines before the main Japanese forces come up, pin down advance units, and cause confusion in rear areas by seizing key positions quickly and boldly.

The British regard it as of the highest importance that these shock troops be dealt with as quickly as possible, by what is termed a "blitz" party. They recommend that this party be commanded by an experienced officer, often the company commander, and in medium jungle country that the party include two light machine guns and three Tommy guns. The party is formed under cover, and moves to a line of departure as near as possible to the area in which the enemy has been located. From this line, the party advances, shooting from the hip, and spraying all possible enemy positions with short automatic bursts, or two or three rounds of rifle fire. The light machine guns should have tracer ammunition. Muzzles are kept well down for ricochet effect. Any houses and trees in the line of advance must be sprayed with fire. In order to avoid loss of contact between elements of the party and to insure a ready supply of ammunition, care must be taken not to advance too far. It is reported that the Japanese will not stand up against shock tactics of this sort. It is further suggested that "blitz" parties should be made up on the spot from available troops at hand rather than organized as specialist groups; if specialist groups are formed it is feared that they will often not be present at the right time or the right place. Therefore, all riflemen should be trained to participate in a tactical group of this sort.

Emphasis is placed on the need for heavy automatic-weapon fire in jungle warfare against the Japanese shock troops. To meet the automatic weapons of the enemy, the heaviest weight of fire power must be used, and used first.

The British report of this campaign expresses the belief that if the Japanese shock troops can be successfully dealt with, there is less to fear from the action of the main forces.

E. JAPANESE PURSUIT

It is reported in this campaign that the Japanese failed noticeably in aggressive pursuit of withdrawing United Nations forces. This failure was presumably due either to orders which limited forces to a particular objective, or else indicated lack of initiative in pursuit tactics.

F. MORTARS IN JUNGLE FIGHTING

The Japanese 4-inch mortar proved a formidable weapon in jungle warfare. It was brought up very quickly after contact was established, and fire was accurate.

The Japanese avoided siting their mortars on the edge of a jungle or wood. They were generally placed well back from the edge, even as far as 400 to 600 yards. This meant that observation posts must have been well forward of the mortar position, and it is thought that these posts must have controlled the fire by light radio sets or by telephone.

It is reported that the Japanese do not stand up well to shell fire and that mortar fire is very effective in silencing Japanese mortar posts or machine-gun posts. The value of searching fire directed against Japanese light machine guns, mortars, and artillery was very noticeable. On many occasions searching fire of 3-inch British mortars, with variations in range, and deflection shifts of 2 to 10 degrees, had the effect of completely silencing enemy positions over long periods. The British give the following recommendations with regard to use of the mortar:

(1) It is an extremely valuable weapon for the jungle, often being the only support weapon which can deal with short-range targets.

(2) Movement of mortars in jungle country presents a serious problem. Except on main roads the mortars cannot be moved by motor transport. Pack mortars are liable to be lost through the stampede of animals under fire. Jeeps are recommended as the ideal transport vehicle.

(3) Even at night, mortars should be sited away from the edges of jungle clearings or isolated woods in order to avoid being spotted by muzzle flash and neutralized by enemy mortars. The Japanese have often been able to locate machine-gun and mortar positions by patrols and then bring accurate fire at night on these positions. The patrols indicate the position of the weapons by converging fire with red tracer ammunition.

(4) In selecting the mortar position, care must be taken to insure a field of fire clear of tree boughs for a wide traverse. A 15-foot screen of foliage in front of the line of fire will screen the muzzle flash.

(5) The observation posts for direction of mortar fire should be

pushed up to the edge of the jungle and should operate by some simple form of visual signal.

(6) The initial laying of the mortar can be accomplished either by the detachment commander at the mortar position, or by sending a gunner forward to the observation post to get range and direction. The opening fire must be at safe margins and corrections boldly made.

(7) In difficult positions, communication from the observation post will be facilitated by clearing tunnels through the jungle. This must be done in such a way as to conceal the tunnels from ground or air observation.

(8) If the rounds fall in high jungle, observation of the fire may be completely blanketed. Where this is the case, systematic searching fire must be used instead of corrected fire.

(9) Smoke ammunition may be used in the jungle to set a dry area on fire, but it is suggested that incendiary ammunition would be much more effective for this purpose.

(10) The small 2-inch mortar is also a good jungle weapon.

JAPANESE OPERATIONAL PRINCIPLES: MANDALAY OFFENSIVE

Tactical and Technical Trends, No. 9, October 8, 1942.

The following document, dated March 26, 1942, was found on the corpse of a Japanese battalion commander, and its importance is indicated by the reminder, over the signature of the Chief of Staff of the Army, to the effect that "this document must be carefully protected."

The document starts out by highlighting the objectives to be sought by the Japanese in this campaign, and goes on to enumerate the several steps necessary to bring about a decisive battle in the Mandalay area.

The full text of the instructions follows:

A. OBJECTIVE

The objective of our Army in this campaign is to crush the combined forces of the British and Chinese, especially the latter. This is to prevent their cooperation, and to consolidate the whole of Burma.

Our army is now fighting to bring about a decisive battle for the South Area Army Forces. Once we succeed, we shall not only check the ambitions of the British in the Far East, but will also deliver a crushing blow to Chiang Kai-Shek's administration, and speed his downfall. Otherwise, if we lack thoroughness in dealing with the enemy, and the battle is a long one, the effect on the Greater East Asia war will be considerable.

All ranks in the army should be taught thoroughly the significance of this campaign and our responsibility.

B. PLAN

Before coming to a general engagement, the army should try to catch and annihilate the enemy in their individual areas. But in general the army should either lure the Chinese army out, or force it to fight in the vicinity of Mandalay. Once this is done, the retreat of the main force must be cut off by a wide encircling movement. Meanwhile the enemy's attention must be held, and our frontal units should hold him from retreating until he is exhausted. Then the whole of our army in close cooperation will catch and destroy the enemy, whether encircled or isolated.

This can be called the fundamental plan of this campaign. However the enemy must also have plans; therefore, our fighting must be maintained according to prevailing conditions. It is of primary importance to fight according to this basic plan in order to attain the objective.

The intended encirclement of the enemy is of the greatest importance. When in contact, it must be found out if there is any possibility of the enemy's evading the encirclement. Here the circumstances are different from the conduct of operations in China. In this country, the local inhabitants are quite friendly to as and hostile to the enemy. Moreover, outside the encirclement areas, the country is rough and mountainous. Apart from the main roads, we can well say that there are no lines of communication. All these factors are handicaps to the enemy, and advantageous to our own fighting services. If there is any sign of the enemy's withdrawing before we are ready to strike, we must lose no time in pursuing them so as to fulfill the objective of our fighting plan.

C. METHODS

The following points are to bring about the above plan, and are to be understood by all units.

(1) In order to complete the encirclement, the following points are to be memorized:

(a) Secrecy

Units that are assigned to build up the encirclement on the outer wing of the enemy's main force, should, before the general offensive of the army, maintain complete secrecy from enemy air or ground observation, by making use of terrain and darkness. Should they encounter the enemy, these units should encircle him and launch an immediate attack, and avoid giving any information which may lead to an estimate of our strength.

There have been many cases in which the enemy has been able to estimate our strength through movements of our troops in the rear. The secrecy of our rear movements must therefore be strictly maintained. Even in other sectors, although units are northward bound, we should not allow the enemy to overestimate our strength, lest this lead to an early withdrawal of the enemy's main force.

(b) Urgency of Mobility

Ultimate success or failure in a battle depends on the mobility of the units that cut off the enemy's retreat. Once the offensive is on the move, then the units assigned to cut off the enemy's retreat must overcome all difficulties and occupy their objective at a given time.

For this purpose, these units should make full use of local transport organizations, but must not rely too much on these to the detriment of our fighting mobility.

When engaging the enemy, it is not essential to engage him frontally. A sudden flank attack will weaken his defense.

Units assigned to cut off the enemy's retreat are specially picked troops. Preparation for their transportation on short notice to their destination should be completed. After starting, these units should proceed directly to their destination if not harassed by the enemy. They must also, when on the march, maintain contact with other units following.

(c) Roads

The enemy is paying great attention to the construction of strong defensive positions on roads, but generally neglects the importance of the area on the sides of the roads.

Generally speaking, the British and Indian troops pay little attention to demolition of roads, as a result of which the thrust of motorized units is found to be particularly effective. Even the Chinese army seldom destroys Burmese roads as they do their own, since the local inhabitants are, generally speaking, hostile to the Chinese, and without the help of local inhabitants, destruction of roads cannot be fully achieved.

(d) Strongpoints

Units that are assigned to cut off the enemy's retreat must immediately consider the protection of the places they have to occupy. At the same time, they must maintain close contact with other units. They must be in a position either to attack the enemy or to defend themselves. Not one of the enemy must be allowed to escape, and the strong points must be held even if the enemy is attempting to break through from an advantageous position.

There is a common tendency among our troops to neglect the construction of strongpoints, especially protection against tanks and aircraft. When a place is to be protected, antitank obstructions should be erected. If engineers are attached, the construction will be more effective.

(e) Mopping-up

Mopping-up operations within the area of encirclement require time; therefore, the removal of troops from the enemy's line of retreat should not be done until the order is given.

(2) Important Points for Mopping-up Operations

(a) Aggressive Spirit

Not one enemy inside the encirclement must be allowed to escape, whether the operation takes 10 or 20 days. Everything to annihilate them must be done, and with no half-way measures.

(b) Use of Fighting Strength

In the campaign, close cooperation between air and ground must be maintained. Our forces must be concentrated according to time and conditions in order to defeat the enemy as quickly as possible. For this, the various signaling units must be suitably employed, and cooperation well planned.

(c) Air and Ground Cooperation

As the encirclement may extend several hundred kilometers, we require the cooperation of air units while the mopping-up is in full swing. During these operations, air and ground strength must be concentrated at one point, and therefore close air and ground cooperation is very essential. Any unit, under any conditions, must at once distinguish whether a plane overhead is ours or the enemy's, and, if ours, give the prearranged recognition signal. Units must not feel disappointed if it happens to be one of the enemy planes.

d. Supplies from the Rear

Owing to the distances that have to be covered, and the rapid movement of first line units, supplies are usually overdue; therefore, provisions for the troops must be found locally. But as regards ammunition, troops must keeps it secure and die with it. If they rely on supplies from the rear they will certainly lose fighting mobility.

e. Use of Local Inhabitants in Fighting Areas

The movements of the natives have a great effect on the outcome of a campaign. Units must exercise good discipline towards them. Propaganda and pacification should be started at the first opportunity, and everything must be done to induce the people to cooperate with us.

As regards the Burmese, we must respect and protect their temples, and thereby induce the monks to help us.

JAPANESE DOCTRINE ON OBSTACLES

Tactical and Technical Trends, No. 10, October 22, 1942.

The following is a summary of a translation of portions of the Japanese Field Fortification Manual:

A. ELECTRICAL OBSTACLES

(1) Principle

Electrified wire is used to cause casualties to men and horses and to hamper hostile attacks.

(2) Construction

Normally, wire is strung on dry poles with bark removed, or on poles with all buried portions insulated with asphalt or coal tar. The bare wire is strung and connected with a high-tension source (1,000 to 2,000 volts AC), so that a person coming in contact with the obstacle wire closes the circuit. Transmission wires may also be strung along the ground, or under ground. (No details of the generating plant are given.)

(3) Use

Ordinarily, the current is not turned on except during actual attacks. A variation consists in electrifying certain sections of the wire during hostile reconnaissance, and electrifying additional sections during the attack.

(4) Reconnaissance of Hostile Electric Obstacles

The Japanese consider it important to locate electrical obstacles prior to an attack. Reconnaissance parties attempt to determine the characteristics of the source of power, and of the transmission lines. The following points are indicative of the presence of electrified obstacles:

- Bark stripped off lower portions of wire obstacle poles.
- Presence of asphalt cloth or other insulation around the buried portions of posts and pegs.
- Any noticeable decrease in the number of wires, posts, and pegs.
- Low wires free from contact with the ground.
- Absence of additional loose barbed wire (used in some cases to strengthen obstacles).
- Presence of insulators or transmission wires.
- Burnt or smoldering grass close to wire lines.
- Sparks when small-arms fire cuts the wire.

(5) Use of Detectors

The Japanese use several types of electrical detectors. One appears to be a simple voltmeter. Another type is a field telephone to pick up earth currents resulting from electric wire at distances of over 100 feet. Also mentioned are a magnetic induction detector with a range up to 1,300 yards, and an improvised detector using a radio receiver amplifier with a range up to 500 yards.

(6) Destruction of Electrical Obstacles

Destruction is accomplished by demolition, wire cutting, and artillery fire. In some cases lines may be shorted by throwing water or brine on the posts. Bangalore torpedoes are the best means of demolition. After the use of both demolitions and artillery fire, loose wire ends are dangerous and must be avoided. Special squads equipped with rubber gloves, rubber boots, wire-cutters, and some type of nets for cutting paths through wire are trained in following up demolition work. No matter what the method of demolition, it is emphasized that a path wide enough for the passage of the attackers must be created, and all loose wire ends must be wrapped around posts. The resulting paths should be clearly marked.

B. MINES AND TRAPS

(1) Mine Detection

The Japanese emphasize the necessity for studying the functioning of enemy mines and the enemy procedure for mine laying. Mine detection is generally a mission of technical troops.

(2) Elements of Detection

A detailed search for enemy mines should include attention to the following:

- Those regions from which the enemy purposely keeps away.
- Presence or absence of sentries.
- Removal of civilians.
- Intelligence re enemy's mine laying.
- Change in color of soil, small swells, and mud cracks.
- Exposures or traces of plates, wire, etc.
- Any trip wire and rope on ground, or roads, or in forests.
- Presence of poles and pegs whose use is unusual.
- Waste paper or packing bits used in mine laying.
- Mechanical noise coming from clock-run delay device.
- Smell of chemical from chemical delay device.
- Connection wire between obstacle and ground.
- Wire connecting abandoned weapons and other booby traps.
- Rocks scattered on roads.
- Wire fastened to doors and windows.

(3) Probing Rods

A mine-detecting rod for probing is mentioned. Lacking other means, spades are employed.

(4) Mine Destruction

The Japanese prefer to remove discovered mines, but on occasion will mark located mine fields or will destroy mines by firing them.

C. ANTITANK OBSTACLES

(1) Types

The Japanese recommend use of the triangular trench, circular pit, and side-hill barriers for antitank defense. In the use of portable obstacles, two tows on level ground and single rows on steep slopes are suggested.

(2) Destruction of Obstacles

The destruction of steel-rail obstacles and side-hill barriers by explosives is recommended. It is suggested that generally it is best to fill trench-and-pit-type obstacles, using crib-work and earth-filled baskets.

Comment:

It is recognized that this particular Japanese text deals with obstacles in a very superficial manner. This summary is presented in order to give a Japanese approach to the obstacle problem. Nothing has occurred in the war thus far to indicate a general Japanese weakness in dealing with mines or obstacles.

JAPANESE DEFENSIVE TACTICS IN THE SOLOMONS

Tactical and Technical Trends, No. 10, October 22, 1942.

The following are notes on Japanese defensive tactics encountered by our forces in recent actions in the Solomon Islands:

"Japanese trenches and shelters on the islands attacked by U.S. forces were skillfully emplaced under buildings and hedges. All dirt excavated in constructing shelters had been carried away so that detection of field works was very difficult.

"Telephone lines of galvanized wire were laid between Japanese strongpoints. Our shell fire and bombing had disrupted their communications, No evidence of visual signalling or arm and hand signals was observed. At night the Japanese used whistle signals, but their meaning was not established.

"Japanese weapons noted were rifles, pistols, light machine guns and grenades. Mortar fire was encountered on some islands but not on others.

"The flanks of Japanese positions and weapon emplacements were covered by snipers. Snipers were concealed in the tops of palm trees and were not detected until they opened fire, despite careful observation of tree tops. The Browning automatic rifle proved to be an excellent weapon for dealing with snipers.

"On several occasions, the Japanese were called upon to surrender but ignored the opportunity. Two Japanese were observed to throw down their rifles and run toward our lines with their hands in the air. Our forces ceased fire, but a Japanese machine gun shot down the would-be prisoners before they reached our lines.

"The Japanese made extensive use of natural caves, and replaced casualties at near-by guns from personnel in reserve in the caves.

"When grenades were first tossed into Japanese positions, the Japs threw them back. It was found necessary by our troops to release the firing mechanism and count to three before throwing, in order that grenades would explode before the Japs could throw them back.

"Fighting took place at ranges of 50 to 100 yards.

"The Japanese staged several small local counterattacks of 8 to 10 men led by an officer. The Japanese were nearly invisible but disclosed their positions by holding their rifles, with fixed bayonets, aloft while they assembled.

"The slit trenches employed by the Japanese gave excellent protection from bombing.

"When questioned about the lack of prisoners, a U.S. officer said that apparently a great deal of propaganda had been spread among the Japanese soldiers about the horrible things that would happen to prisoners.

"Naval gunfire and dive-bombing was still going on when the initial wave landed. No fire was received by this first wave, as all the Japanese had taken cover. After cessation of naval gun fire and bombing, the Japanese began firing from dugouts on the island and fire was received from an adjacent island.

"The first wave tossed grenades into the entrance to the dugouts that they passed. Although the grenades exploded within the entrance, it was later found that they were ineffective due to the type of entryway. Enemy troops fired from dugouts on the rear of the first wave and into the second and third waves, aided by snipers in the tops of coconut trees.

"Japanese dugouts were cut back into the hill on the island and were faced on the front and flanks with sand bags and steel plates. A U.S. sergeant sketched one of these dugouts as follows:

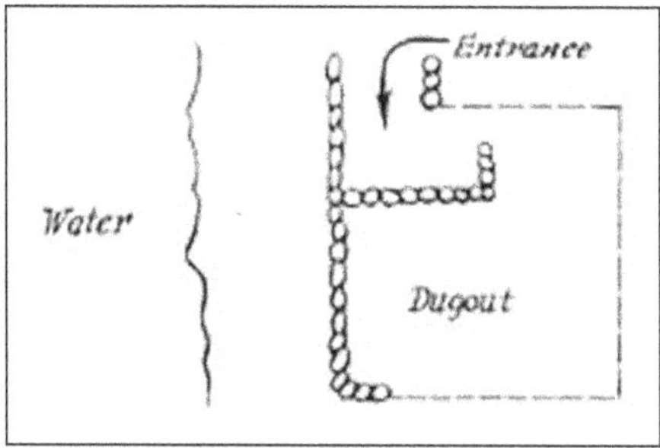

"The Sergeant stated that the Japanese fired from the entry of the dugout. Each dugout had about eight men in it.

"Fourteen dugouts were seen by the sergeant. He stated they were close to the water's edge and were mutually supporting.

"The Japanese installed no obstacles nor rigged any booby traps.

"One double-barreled light machine gun was captured. It fed alternately right and left from a central clip.

"The Japanese were very adept at concealing themselves. Some hid under their shelter halves and others under fallen palm fronds. One sniper shot down from a tree had coconuts hung around his neck to help conceal him. One sniper in a palm tree had protected himself with armor plate.

"No means of communication between dugouts were seen nor did the sergeant see any control exercised by officers or noncommissioned officers. Soldiers appeared to fight as individuals.

"Japanese marksmanship was characterized as poor and not very dangerous if one kept moving and avoided lying in the open.

"It was emphasized that no flash, smoke or muzzle blast was visible from Japanese weapons and this materially aided the Japanese in remaining concealed.

"The Japanese snipers paid particular attention to picking off officers and noncommissioned officers whose exterior garments carried insignia or markings indicating their rank."

* * * *

Further information on the Solomon Islands campaign and on the tactics and fighting qualities of the Japanese soldier is contained in the following abstract of a personal letter from a Marine officer serving with our forces in the Solomons.

"I want to try and describe some of the characteristics of the Japanese soldier. Some of it may sound like so much hooey but it is an actual fact.

"Individually, he is a good soldier; in fact, an excellent one. They very, very seldom give up but will fight until killed, even after being badly wounded. Of a force of well over 700 that we wiped out, we were only able to take 34 prisoners, and 33 of them were so badly wounded that they couldn't do anything. We asked each one if they had been told that they would be killed if captured and they said "No," but that they expected to be. All insisted that they would never be able to return to Japan, so that probably is the answer.

"The first bunch that hit my right flank at 3 a.m. on the 21st, evidently didn't realize that they were approaching our positions. They were walking right in the edge of the surf and got tangled up in some barbwire that we had salvaged from fences. They started jabbering so our bunch let go with everything they had. They immediately rushed our positions and it was a grand mess for a few minutes. After driving them from our positions they took refuge right in the edge of the surf underneath a 3-foot bank and there they stayed about 50 yards from our line. By that time their main force closed in and tried to advance down the narrow sandspit; naturally, the slaughter was terrific. The rest of the main body had deployed on the east side of the river—about 100 yards from our lines—and a beautiful fire fight continued for many hours. They were well equipped with mortars, 70-mm cannons, flame-throwers, and heavy machine guns.

"There were probably close to 200 that were actually piled up along the narrow sandspit. The ones that were wounded would lie perfectly still but continued to snipe at us all during the day. We had one captain wounded by one even after we had, we thought, cleaned them out thoroughly. As we closed in through the mass of bodies, one man happened to step on a hand and he thought he felt it move so he kicked it. As he did, the Jap jumped up and tried to throw a grenade at a group near but the pin never came out. I actually saw dead Japs with grenades in their hands with the pins pulled. Others that I saw had two or three wounds that had been bound up, but they stayed right there until the end.

"After it was all over, we saw one swimming well out to sea so we sent a boat out to get him. As the boat came alongside he made a dive and never came up. In other words, they kill or get killed. You must give them that credit.

"As you have been told before, they are great on sniping. After our initial landing, and after they had taken to the mountains, they worried us quite a bit, as they would slip in at night (or hide out during the day) and do a lot of firing. For two nights we actually had them running around inside Regimental Headquarters lines. As it was as dark as pitch we couldn't fire and they would outrun our boys. We had one sniper near our galley that would take one shot of a morning and one in the evening. We combed the fields and the coconut trees but we never found him. I am glad to say that he was a damn poor shot and he didn't get anyone before he finally beat it.

"Each Jap carried a camouflage net made of mesh with wood-fiber strands, and it is actually impossible to see them at 50 yards if they lie still with it on.

"The unit that hit us had landed 40 miles down the beach two nights before, so they had hiked and carried all of their heavy equipment that distance in less than 22 hours' hiking time. They hid in the brush during daylight. They had no food except what little each man carried and it was practically nil—I imagine they had eaten what they brought ashore and I can't figure out what they expected to do for more. Maybe they expected to get ours.

"In my opinion it boils down to this. The Japs are excellent individual soldiers but their headwork is very poor. They have gotten away with murder so many times maybe they think that it only takes a small force to lick a big one. Well, they got badly fooled once anyway."

JAPANESE PRISONERS OF WAR

Tactical and Technical Trends, No. 10, October 22, 1942.

In the last issue of Tactical and Technical Trends an article appeared on the methods of dealing with German prisoners of war as reported in a personal letter written by a British Intelligence Officer in the North African desert. Some interesting observations on this question concerning Japanese PW are brought out in the report which follows.

* * * *

Though it is true that the experiences gained from interrogating Japanese PW have not been as numerous as in the case of the Germans or Italians, nevertheless, it has been possible to indicate a pattern of behavior. However, no hard and fast rules can be made, since the problems of interrogation are as varied as human nature itself, and each case has to be treated on its merits. National and personal idiosyncrasies must be taken into account, and it is almost literally true that one PW's food is another's poison.

Such a contingency as capture by the enemy is not recognized by the Japanese military authorities. It is carefully inculcated into the Japanese soldier that to allow himself to be captured is a disgrace worse than death. Indeed, to some extent, he even welcomes the chance to die for his country. "Meet you at Yasukuni" is a popular parting expression used by a Japanese soldier to a comrade when leaving for the front. Yasukuni is a shrine in Tokyo where the ashes of "fallen heroes" are enshrined and paid homage to by millions every year.

The Japanese is therefore a difficult fish to catch. He will resist to the last... Moreover, unauthenticated reports from Malaya mentioned cases of Japanese pilots who made successful forced landings, but blew out their brains before they could be disarmed.

According to the account of one Japanese PW, the Japanese troops who had been captured in Russia during the Nomonhan incident in 1939, and afterwards returned to Japan, were given a knife with which to commit "hara-kiri." Names of "missing" Japanese soldiers are officially reported as "killed," and their names removed from the family registers. Indeed, urns containing cremated ashes may be sent to their next of kin as proof that the "missing" are no longer alive.

Schooled in the code of honor which requires suicide rather than capture, the Japanese cannot easily be taken prisoner. Even after capture under circumstances entirely beyond his control, (e.g. a pilot who has crashed, and regained consciousness only in hospital), the well-trained Japanese officer may still demand a pistol to shoot himself, though this attitude then smacks somewhat of a theatrical flourish to save face. But once beyond the reach of help and the immediate opportunity of self-destruction, a complete mental reconstruction is not uncommon.

The following incident shows the typical attitude of the PW as soon as the self-destruction phase passes.

One Japanese interrogated in Melbourne said he had no desire to return to Japan. He believed that his former friends would have nothing to do with him because he had been taken alive by the enemy and that he would be unable to get back into the army. He preferred to stay in Australia.

Coupled with the comparative leniency of his captors, this conviction induces in the prisoner a pliancy unusual in PW's from other nations, say, Nazi Germany. The self-justification is: "Officially, I am dead; legally, I am stateless: why not talk if I can thereby mitigate or improve my position with my captors."

In other words, his security has been more a matter of external training than of inner conviction. In an entirely new environment the traditional supports of his loyalty fall away and leave him ready to answer most questions, though he does occasionally salve his conscience by showing unwillingness to reveal matters which, in his own words, he describes as "firing a bullet at the heart of the Emperor." The names of his superior officers are revealed with reluctance.

The above remarks apply particularly to Japanese officers, who have been given some instruction on security. So far as the rank and file are concerned, they do not seem to realize that by talking they may be betraying their comrades. This serves to emphasize the necessity of segregating officers from other troops, as soon after capture as possible. Segregation should be arranged immediately and prisoners sent back to the next higher echelon under separate guard.

Aside from officers, information has been forthcoming from straight-forward interrogation. Although the Japanese soldier may prefer death to capture, yet, when captured, he has been a valuable source of information.

This should be pointed out to all troops, and the importance of preserving and sending back documents captured with the prisoner should also be stressed. The Intelligence Officer's task is greatly facilitated if he has been able to examine relevant documents before he does his interrogation. As regards the treatment of prisoners when captured, it is very understandable that troops in the heat of battle cannot be expected to be overgentle, but if it is explained to them that prisoners are more amenable when treated well, they will be prepared to cooperate. They should be made to realize that from the intelligence point of view one live Japanese is worth more than fifty dead ones.

One PW disclosed that he had been told of the capture of a British pilot who, though subjected to an intense interrogation, had refused to talk at all. When asked as to what measures the Japanese would be likely to take with a prisoner of this description, he said he was certain that no attempt would be made to extract information by third-degree methods, as the Japanese nature was such as to admire reticence on the part of a soldier.

Comment: It is evident that this particular PW was indulging in some artful practices in order to secure better treatment for himself.

FURTHER NOTES ON THE BURMA CAMPAIGN

Tactical and Technical Trends, No. 11, November 5, 1942.

The following are some further items from British sources on the experiences gained in the Burma Campaign. Other material on this subject was included in Tactical and Technical Trends, No. 9, p. 15.

A. PACE OF FIGHTING

The British reports stress the "absolute necessity" for an adequate flow of reinforcements, permitting the interchange of units in the front line so that troops will have a rest every 3 or 4 days. The Japanese Army (it is stated), will sacrifice manpower and use fresh troops in repeated assaults to gain an objective.

B. ARMING OF SERVICE TROOPS

In the fighting in Burma, lines of communication were very long and exposed, and the Japanese made dangerous attacks on rear areas by flanking or infiltration groups. Under these conditions, it was regarded as absolutely necessary that all types of troops—engineer, signal corps, ordnance, etc.—should be provided with, and trained in the use of, rifle, bayonet, grenades, machine guns, and Tommy guns.

C. EQUIPMENT FOR JUNGLE FIGHTING

The following recommendations were made:

(1) Troops should be armed at all times. Every man should be issued a bandolier, which he can carry about with his rifle wherever he goes. Full equipment need not be worn at all times; in an emergency the important thing is to have a rifle

and 50 rounds.

(2) Every man should carry at least one light machine-gun magazine in addition to his own ammunition.

(3) Some form of knife should be issued to troops in jungle country.

(4) Individual entrenching tools should be carried by every one, but should be modified to exclude the pick end and to make the digging end slightly stronger (Note: this refers to British types of tools). These would be supplemented in the battalion by ordinary picks and shovels.

D. INFANTRY PATROLS

(1) Length of Patrols

Throughout the Burma Campaign, infantry were at all times called upon for heavy patrol duties. The number and length of patrols were increased by the enclosed nature of the country (restricting observation), by lack of reconnaissance aircraft, shortage of mobile troops, and the Japanese aptitude for using little known and even unmarked trails. The arrival of an armored brigade did little to help reduce the burden put on the infantry; in the early stages, this brigade operated as a separate mobile force ahead of the infantry, and later was employed for shock action or distant patrolling.

These factors not only made patrol duties heavy, but increased beyond ordinary requirements the depth to which patrols were required to operate. Bren-carrier patrols to a distance of 13 miles were commonplace, and sometimes infantry on foot were called upon to patrol as far as 15 miles ahead of forward units. The necessity for frequent carrier patrols, at long distances, led to the carrier vehicles being treated as armored cars—an unsuitable role. Many were lost on roads and trails in close country through grenade or mortar attacks, or through destruction of the crew by snipers armed with automatic weapons and concealed in trees.

(2) Functioning of Patrols

When infantry patrols are sent on foot for such long distances from their nearest support, very high morale is required, as well as leadership above the average. If a patrol returns prematurely or fails to carry out its mission, this may vitally affect the security of the main forces.

In a country where Fifth Columnists are numerous, British sources recommend special precautions, such as moving only at night and avoiding villages.

(3) Forms of Patrols

In some cases, infantry in trucks accompanied armored carriers on long-distance patrols. It is doubted whether this was good practice, since the infantry was vulnerable to attack and the trucks had limited capacities for cross-country patrol work.

On one occasion, a 3-inch mortar was man-handled forward by a patrol and achieved a notable success, the enemy being completely unprepared for fire of this type forward of the British positions.

(4) Sending Back Information

Lack of equipment for communications added to the difficulties of patrol work in close country. Information was often slow in getting back from the patrols. Retirements of the main forces often had to be made on short notice, and patrols could not always be notified of the movement. Sound signals (prearranged fires, etc.) were not always a practical method of overcoming this difficulty.

(5) Possible Use of Cavalry

Neither side employed cavalry for patrols. The British report suggests that cavalry using small native ponies would have been invaluable in this campaign. For patrol work, it is suggested that the mounted infantry should have a high proportion of light machine guns and submachine guns carried with the troops. Mounted patrols could use pack wireless and Jeeps to communicate information and receive orders. Specifically, the report suggests that three companies of mounted infantry, plus a company of armored scout cars (U.S. type) having some heavy mortars, would make the ideal reconnaissance unit or light covering force for a division.

(6) Maps

Without adequate maps, long distance patrols found great trouble in carrying out assignments in difficult country.

E. VILLAGE FIGHTING

Village fighting was involved in a majority of the actions in this campaign.

(1) Character of Burmese Villages

They consist of bamboo houses, with the living quarters raised off the ground and entered by a ladder. Cattle and equipment are kept on the ground underneath. The roofs are thatched with leaves, and holes can be easily made in them. Houses are generally separated from each other by bamboo stockades, often with sharpened ends, and the whole village is usually surrounded by a stockade. Cactus hedges are common. Villages, if lacking in bamboo or other cover, are usually built in squares. Where cover is abundant, the village is irregular. There is plenty of cover for concealment in the ordinary village.

Village sanitation is deplorable. The best water supply (wells) was usually in the villages; this led to troop concentrations in or near villages, and so to village fighting. The best water is found at the village temple.

(2) Japanese Tactics

The Japanese shock-troops were adept at infiltrating into villages and concealing themselves. They used trees extensively; also green camouflage nets. They were skillful in taking cover in houses and frequently used the roof as a sniping position, after knocking out a small hole, by supporting themselves on rafters. Culverts, bridges, sunken roads, bamboo clumps, wicker baskets, rice dumps, trenches under houses—all were likely hiding places.

(3) British Tactics

To clear a village occupied by the Japanese required bold and resolute leadership. The roads were to be avoided. Unless the village ran into the jungle, a straightforward advance through the houses on both sides of the road paid best. Attack, in two waves, should include a firing party with automatic weapons followed by a mopping-up party—both with plenty of bombs.

If snipers were not caught by the first wave, they could be dealt with by setting fire to houses and other cover—in such a way as not to interfere with the main operation. Mopping-up had to be thorough, and the houses searched from ground to roof; otherwise, the Jap merely "fades out" and "fades in" again at will. When the village is flanked with jungle, it is suicidal for attacking troops to advance across the more open spaces of the village with the flanks not cleared. An encircling movement through the jungle into the village will bring fewer casualties. In such a maneuver, objectives must be strictly limited. As each successive objective is gained, there must be a pause for reorganization, selection of the best objective (to be clearly stated to all troops), and replenishment of ammunition. These encircling movements can be supported by frontal covering fire with automatic weapons.

Tanks can be effectively used in support of infantry in clearing a village. They advance down roads echeloned back from each wave of infantry. They are thus comparatively safe from antitank grenades, and the infantry ahead of the tanks can deal with antitank weapons covering the road. Tanks often obtained a favorable target by moving along the flanks of villages.

Armored carriers can be used in a similar way, if tanks are not available. Both tanks and carriers can easily make breaches in stockades by charging them.

(4) Miscellaneous

The searching fire of mortars, well in front of advancing infantry, is effective in making the Japanese give ground.

In firing a village (to improve fields of fire), it should be remembered that dumps of rice will take 2 to 3 days to burn out. A dry bamboo house will burn out in 20 to 30 minutes. The "plop" of burning bamboo shoots has often been mistaken for enemy small-arms fire.

SOME EXAMPLES OF KATAKANA (PHONETIC JAPANESE) USED IN COMMUNICATIONS

Tactical and Technical Trends, No. 12, November 19, 1942.

This article is presented for the purpose of clarifying some of the mystery in which, to the layman, the Japanese language is shrouded. Also, it is to be hoped that it will stimulate some interest in the language, especially on the part of communications personnel.

It must be pointed out that there exist no short cuts enabling one to acquire a comprehensive knowledge of this language. Years of unremitting labor are required to master even the fundamentals of writing Japanese kanji (the classic language, which is basically Chinese); however, kana, or phonetic Japanese writing, can be learned in a short time. Communications personnel may, with practice, intercept and transcribe some portions of coded messages which use kana.

A. THE JAPANESE WRITTEN LANGUAGE

(1) Chinese Characters (Kanji)

It was not until the fourth or fifth century of the Christian era that the Japanese felt the need of putting down their thoughts in writing. They had no alphabet, and since their only intercourse with the then known world was with China to the west, they proceeded to borrow, along with many other things, their writing system from that country.

The Chinese writing system is about as difficult a thing to learn or to use as man's mind has ever invented. It started out being a sort of picture language with each word represented by a simplified picture. This system was all right for words like "horse" or "fish," words that could be drawn, but it would not do for more abstract words like "duty," "courage," or "honesty." Obviously, the writing system had to develop far beyond simple pictures, which it did more than 3,000 years ago. But Chinese writing never lost some of its original pictorial quality. There still is one symbol, if not picture, for each word. As a result, there are thousands of symbols, or characters, as they are usually called, in use today in China.

The Chinese system was not a handy one for the Japanese to borrow, but it was all they knew. They had to supplement it with other written signs (kana), developed by themselves, which showed sounds, the way our alphabet does, and not ideas, the way the Chinese characters do. But even after inventing these phonetic writing systems, they still kept to the Chinese characters. They were pronounced quite differently in Japan than in China, because the two spoken languages are not at all alike, but still they represented the same idea. Consequently, most Chinese words can be read and understood by Japanese, and many Japanese words can be read and understood by Chinese. This is not true for pronunciation.

(2) Phonetic Characters (Kana: Katakana and Hiragana)

In katakana and hiragana each character represents a sound, but, unlike English letters, each is made up of a consonant followed by a vowel, i.e., ka, ki, etc. Exceptions are the vowels a, e, i, o, u, and the consonant n. The katakana consists of 50 somewhat angular symbols which, apart from their use on aircraft, are used by the Japanese mainly for transcribing foreign sounds, and in notices, official documents, telegrams, ships' names, etc. Inscriptions in katakana are usually written from the right, either vertically or horizontally, but on occasions are written from left to right as in English. The hiragana syllabary compares with katakana as our script letters (a) compare with block printing (A). It also consists of 50 forms, but they are cursive in shape and are used in writing letters, in some newspapers, etc. These characters are seldom used for aircraft markings or for depicting ships' names.

In writing out the kana sounds in our alphabet, the following rules are invariably used.

a	ア	as in father
i	イ	as in machine
u	ウ	as oo in loot
e	エ	as a in hay
o	オ	as in oh

A table of the characters used in the katakana syllabary follows:

ア a	カ ka	サ sa	タ ta	ナ na	ハ ha	マ ma	ヤ ya	ラ ra	ワ wa	
イ i	キ ki	シ shi	チ chi	ニ ni	ヒ hi	ミ mi	イ i	リ ri	ヰ (w)i	
ウ u	ク ku	ス su	ツ tsu	ヌ nu	フ fu	ム mu	ユ yu	ル ru	ウ u	ン n
エ e	ケ ke	セ se	テ te	ネ ne	ヘ he	メ me	エ (y)e	レ re	ヱ (w)e	
オ o	コ ko	ソ so	ト to	ノ no	ホ ho	モ mo	ヨ yo	ロ ro	ヲ wo	

Sometimes katakana symbols are used with Japanese numerals and the result is confusing. The katakana for se (SYMBOL) and for ha (SYMBOL) look confusingly like the numerals shichi (SYMBOL) seven, and hachi (SYMBOL), eight.

Sometimes katakana symbols are used with Japanese numerals and the result is confusing. The katakana for se (セ) and for ha (ハ) look confusingly like the numerals shichi (七) seven, and hachi (八), eight.

0	〇	rei
1	一	ichi
2	二	ni
3	三	san
4	四	shi
5	五	go
6	六	roku
7	七	shichi
8	八	hachi
9	九	ku
10	十	ju (to)

Exceptions: By placing two dots called nigori to the right of the character, a hardened and slightly different consonant sound is produced. The ha column becomes ba, bi, bu, be, bo; the ta column, da, ji, zu, de, do; the sa column, za, ji, zu, ze, zo; the ka column, ga, gi, gu, ge, go. Thus カ (ka) becomes ガ (ga), etc. A small circle (called hannigori) on the right side of the characters alters the reading to a softer sound. For instance, if placed on the right hand side of the ha column, ha (ハ) becomes パ and represents the sound pa. Hi (ヒ) becomes pi (ピ), etc.

Exceptions: By placing two dots called nigori to the right of the character, a hardened and slightly different consonant sound is produced. The ha column becomes ba, bi, bu, be, bo; the ta column, da, ji, zu, de, do; the sa column, za, ji, zu, ze, zo; the ka column, ga, gi, gu, ge, go. Thus SYMBOL (ka) becomes SYMBOL (ga), etc. A small circle (called hannigori) on the right side of the characters alters the reading to a softer sound. For instance, if placed on the right hand side of the ha column, ha (SYMBOL) becomes SYMBOL and represents the sound pa. Hi (SYMBOL) becomes pi (SYMBOL), etc.

B. APPLICATION OF KATAKANA TO AIRCRAFT

As most Japanese aircraft are marked with characters from the katakana syllabary, it is essential that intelligence officers should have some knowledge of the characters used. In aircraft markings, the katakana syllabary is mainly used; therefore, should a float plane crash or be sighted bearing the under-mentioned markings -

ナガラー

upon referring to the katakana syllabary it would be observed that the first symbol represented the sound na, the second ga, and the third ra; the assembled syllables give "Nagara," the name of a Japanese cruiser. It would, therefore, be established that the float plane was from this cruiser, and that the cruiser was probably in the vicinity. The dash after the character for ra simply indicates a prolonged sound.

C. MAPS AND MAPPING

Since katakana is phonetic, the Japanese use this syllabary to represent most foreign place names except common geographical names which are written in kanji. This fact makes it possible, with a knowledge of katakana, to read most Japanese maps excepting those of either Japan or China. The following are examples of geographical names written in katakana.

Katakana	Romaji or Romanization	English
ブリスベン	(Bu-ri-su-be-n)	Brisbane
ソロモンス	(So-ro-mo-n-su)	Solomons
カーペンタリヤ	(Ka-pe-n-ta-ri-ya)	Carpentaria

An interesting example of the use of katakana in connection with Japanese maps recently came to light in the discovery of some maps together with a canvas bag labelled in Japanese "Reconnaissance Satchel," containing documents and found floating on the sea near the place of crash of a Japanese heavy bomber in the Southwest Pacific area.

A few days later, a mutilated body was washed ashore at about the same place, on which a small diary and note-book and other documents were found. The documents on the body established the identity and the rank of the man, who was a Naval Shosa - i.e., Squadron Leader or Lieutenant Commander. It is also clear from the documents that he had been a Hikocho - i.e., Flying Leader of a Naval Air Group, up to April 1, 1942, when he became attached to an Air Group.

One of the maps is inscribed Hikocho in one place, and in equivalent symbols on another part of the map. This suggests that the maps were almost certainly in the custody of this man.

One of the maps had written on it the name of a flight sergeant whose card was found among the documents in the reconnaissance satchel. It appears, therefore, that the Hikocho was responsible for the maps and all the documents it contained.

Among the maps were:

- 1 Naval Air Headquarters secret map,
- 5 Hydrographic section maps,
- 3 Naval air navigation charts,
- 4 Hydrographic survey charts.

The following general points of interest are disclosed by the maps:

(a) The Japanese had a series of secret maps, covering the eastern part of New Guinea and the Solomon Islands. One captured secret map shows that the Japanese had considerable knowledge of "secret" information about a certain island.

(b) One map gives detailed information of airdromes, anchorages, buildings, radio stations, gun emplacements, repair facilities, the numbers and types of inhabitants, and the availability of gas, food, and water in a certain South

Pacific area.

(c) For the purpose of reference, several of the maps are gridded in pencil. The grid lines are drawn from north to south and from east to west at intervals of 20', and each interval from north to south and from east to west is marked with katakana syllables, sometimes with a pair of syllables. The katakana syllables appear to follow a sequence which sometimes corresponds to the sequence in which the katakana characters appear in the Japanese syllabary given above and sometimes follow the sequence in which they are found in a well-known Japanese poem called the "Iroha song." The poem includes all the katakana syllables. To say that a man knows his Iroha uta is to say that he knows his ABC's.

The Katakana Syllabary in the Iroha uta arrangement follows. The characters are given here in sequence as they occur in the poem.

The first row of characters in each column is the katakana; the second row is Romaji (Japanese for Roman letters); and the third row is the code, dot and dash equivalents.

U, we, wi, and o are sometimes omitted from the sequences used; in one case o is used instead of wo. It is not yet apparent when or how the two sequences are used, nor is it clear what the starting point is of each sequence on the maps. It may be that the starting paint is an arbitrary one fixed on the map and that the two maps are similarly marked for use on a particular occasion or occasions, one map being left at the base and the other taken into the air for the purpose of reference in communication during a flight.

イ	i	·–	ル	ru··	–·––·	ナ	na	·–·
ロ	ro	·–·–	ヲ	wo	·–––	ラ	ra	···
ハ	ha	–···	ワ	wa	–·–	ム	mu	–
ニ	ni	–·–·	カ	ka	·–··	ウ	u	··–
ホ	ho	–··	ヨ	yo	––	ヰ	wi	·–··–
ヘ	he	·	タ	ta	–·	ノ	no	··––
ト	to	··–··	レ	re	–––	オ	o	·–···
チ	chi (ti)	··–·	ソ	so	–––·	ク	ku	···–
リ	ri	––·	ツ	tsu (tu)	·––·	ヤ	ya	·––
ヌ	nu	····	ネ	ne	––·–	マ	ma	–··–
ケ	ke	–·––	キ	ki	–·–··	モ	mo	–··–·
フ	fu	––··	ユ	yu	–··––	セ	se	·–––·
コ	ko	––––	メ	me	–···–	ス	su	–––·–
エ	e	–·–––	ミ	mi	··–·–	ン	n	·–·–·
テ	te	·–·––	シ	shi (si)	––·–·	゛		(nigori)
ア	a	––·––	ヱ	we	·––··	゜		··––· (hannigori)
サ	sa	–·–·–	ヒ	hi	––··–	ー		·––·– (long sound)

(d) As stated, the grid intervals cover 20' of latitude and longitude respectively. For the purpose of subdividing these intervals for closer reference, the maps on which the grids are marked contain a key which in one case subdivides 4 of the grid squares into 16, each square being subdivided into 4 smaller ones. In the other instance, the same principle is followed, but the illustration of it covers 16 of the primary grid squares instead of 16 subsidiary squares, the primary squares not having been subdivided for the purpose of the illustration.

The grid map illustrates the employment of katakana as arranged in normal sequence. The same method of marking has been found on other captured maps.

	167° 0'E.		167° 20'	167° 40'E.
20° 20' S.				
	ア a	イ i	カ ka	キ ki
	1		2	
	ウ u	エ e	ク ku	ケ ke
20° 0'				
	サ sa	シ shi	タ ta	チ chi
	3		4	
	ス su	セ se	ツ tsu	テ te
19° 40'				

D. COMMUNICATIONS IN CODE

When the kana syllabary is used in radio or telegraphic communications, katakana is habitually employed. It should be remembered that this is the printed or typewritten form, and that the receiver of the message, when transcribing the code, would use hiragana. This corresponds to ordinary penmanship as compared to the typewritten or printed letter.

(1) Kana Code Signals with Morse Equivalents

The following is a list indicating Japanese kana code signals with the Morse equivalents. The last two signals on the list (i, ··, nigori) and (un, ··—·, hannigori) are not kana signals, but are used to change the initial consonant of certain kana from the values in column 3 to those of columns 4 or 5. They always follow the kana. For example: -··· is ha, -··· ·· is ba, -··· ··—· is pa. Unless operators are trained in kana reception the above would be copied as follows: -··· as b, -··· ·· as b i, and -··· ··—· as b un.

As previously shown, nigori is indicated in kana characters by the sign (“) placed to the right of the character, and hannigori by the sign (°) also placed to the right of the character.

	Morse	Kana	Romaji	Nigori	Hannigori
a	·–	イ	i		
aa	·–·–	ロ	ro		
ar	·–·–·	ン	n		
as	·–···	オ	o		
au	·–··–	ヰ	wi		
aw	·–·––	テデ	te	de	
b	–···	ハバパ	ha	ba	pa
bt	–···–	メ	me		
d	–·–·	ニ	ni		
c	–··	ホボポ	ho	bo	po

	Morse	Kana	Romaji	Nigori	Hannigori
dm	–··––	ユ	yu		
dn	–··–·	モ	mo		
e	·	ヘベペ	he	be	pe
f	··–·	チヂ	chi (ti)	ji (di)	
g	––·	リ	ri		
h	····	ヌ	nu		
id	··–··	トド	to	do	
j	·–––	ヲ	(w) o		
k	–·–	ワ	wa		
ka	–·–·–	サザ	sa	za	
ki	–·–··	キギ	ki	gi	
km	–·–––	エ	e		
kn	–·––·	ル	ru		
l	·–··	カガ	ka	ga	
m	––	ヨ	yo		
mk	–––·–	スズ	su	zu	
mm	––––	コゴ	ko	go	
mn	–––·	ソゾ	so	zo	
mr	––·–·	シジ	shi (si)	ji (zi)	
mu	––··–	ヒビピ	hi	bi	pi
mw	––·––	ア	a		
n	–·	タダ	ta	da	
o	–––	レ	re		
p	·––·	ツヅ	tsu (tu)	zu (du)	

	Morse	Kana	Romaji	Nigori	Hannigori
q	−−·−	ネ	ne		
r	·−·	ナ	na		
s	···	ラ	ra		
t	−	ム	mu		
u	··−	ウ	u		
ua	··−·−	ミ	mi		
ut	··−−	ノ	no		
v	···−	ク グ	ku	gu	
w	·−−	ヤ	ya		
wi	·−−··	ヱ	(w) e		
wn	·−−−·	セ ゼ	se	ze	
x	−··−	マ	ma		
y	−·−−	ケ ゲ	ke	ge	
z	−−··	フ ブ プ	fu (hu)	bu	pu
i	··	゛	nigori		
un	··−−·	゜	hannigori		

(2) Code Signals for Numerals

The following is the list of code signals employed for the transmission of numerals. The normal signals, abbreviated signals, and the romanized rendering of the Japanese sound occasionally used for number representation during communication are listed, as well as Morse and kana equivalents:

	Morse	Kana	Romaji	Normal	Abbreviated	Romanization
n	−·	タ (一)	ta−1	·−−−−	−·	hi
z	−−··	フ (二)	fu (hu)−2	··−−−	−−··	fu (hu)
s	···	ラ (三)	ra−3	···−−	···	mi
m	−−	ヨ (四)	yo−4	····−	−−	yo
a	·−	イ (五)	i−5	·····	·−	i
t	−	ム (六)	mu−6	−····	−	mu
r	·−·	ナ (七)	na−7	−−···	·−·	na
w	·−−	ヤ (八)	ya−8	−−−··	·−−	ya
v	···−	ク (九)	ku−9	−−−−·	···−	ku
o	−−−	レ (〇)	re−0	−−−−−	−−−	re

(3) Code Signals for Punctuation

Following is a list of auxiliary signals used for punctuation, etc.:

Period	·· ·· ··
Paragraph	·–·–··
Parenthesis (open)	–·––·–
Parenthesis (closed)	·–··–·
Long sound	·––·–
End of message	···–·
Code or abbreviated numerals	––··––
End of part (interrogation)	··––··
End of transmission	···–·–

(4) Abbreviation and Procedure Signals

Following is a list of some of the abbreviations and procedure signals:

	Morse	Kana	Romaji	Meaning
ahr	·–·····–·	イヌナ	i nu na	Here is a message. (I shall continue transmission.)
as	·–···	オ	o	Wait.
asmn	·–···–––·	オソ	o so	Send slower.
awk	·–·–––·–	テワ	te wa	Switch to telephone.
dq	–··––·–	ホネ	ho ne	Break sign. (Body of message follows.)

	Morse	Kana	Romaji	Meaning
eeeeeee	·······			Error.
e a	··–	ヘイ	he i	Close station.
gt	––·–	リム	ri mu	Government telegram.
gw	––··––	リヤ	ri ya	Will use abbreviations or code.
ar	·–·–·	イナ	i na	No, negative.
k	–·–	ワ	wa	Go ahead.
kas	–·–···	サラ	sa ra	Repeat entire message. (Will repeat.)
lar	·–···–·–·	カン	kan	Readability.
larm	·–··–··–·––	カンヨ	kan yo	Good readability, can read.
larmu	·–···–·–·––··–	カンヒ	kan hi	Poor readability, cannot read.
lart	·–···–·–·–	カンム	kan mu	Cannot hear.
mmar	––––·–·–·	コン	kon	Jamming, interference, static.
m	––	ヨ	yo	Local.
rwni	·–··–––···	ナセ	na se (na ze)	Why.
r	·–·	ナ	na	Understood, received.
mrmw	––·–·––·––	シア	shi a (si a)	I have traffic.
mrr	––·–··–·	シナ	shi na (si na)	I have no traffic.
ur	··–·–·	ウナ	u na	Urgent.
uy	··––·––	ウケ	u ke	I have a message for you.
ud	··––··	ウホ	u ho	Interrogation.
umm	··–––––	ウコ	u ko	Receiver.

	Morse	Kana	Romaji	Meaning
ve	···–·			End of message.
x	–··–	マ	ma	Relay message.
mmr	––––·–·	ヨシ	yo shi (yo si)	Yes, affirmative.
zw	––···––	フヤ	fu ya (hu ya)	Transmission not clear.
zz	––··––··	フフ	fu fu (hu hu)	Code signal is not clear.

(5) *Airman's Code of Abbreviations*

The following is a list of the Japanese airman's code of two-syllable abbreviations of military terms. Each abbreviation requires exactly two Japanese Morse signs. The code words Hara and Ware are substitutions and such words as Naru and Yuku are given arbitrary meanings. The list dates from September 1939, but it is believed to be still in common use.

Full Expression	Abbreviation	Katakana	Equivalent	Code	Translation
Gun	kun	クン	ku n	···– ·–·–·	army
Shidan	shita	シタ	shi ta	––·–· –·	division
Ryodan	riyo	リヨ	ri yo	––· ––	brigade
Rentai	ren	レン	re n	––– ·–·–·	regiment
Daitai	tai	タイ	ta i	–· ·–	battalion
Chutai	chu	チウ	chi u	··–· ··–	ccmpany
Shireibu	shire	シレ	shi re	––·–· –––	headquarters
Hohei	hohe	ホヘ	ho he	–·· ·	infantry
Yaho	yaho	ヤホ	ya ho	·–– –··	field artillery
Juho	shiho	シホ	shi ho	––·–· –··	heavy (med) artillery
Kihei	kihe	キヘ	ki he	–·–·· ·	cavalry
Hohei	hou	ホウ	ho u	–·· ··–	artillery

Full Expression	Abbrevi-ation	Kata-kana	Equiva-lent	Code	Translation
Koshaho	koho	コホ	ko ho	---- -..	AA artillery
Shicho	shichi	シチ	shi chi	--.-. ..-.	transport
Kikanju	kika	キカ	ki ka	-.-.. .-..	machine gun
Hikoki	Hiko	ヒコ	hi ko	--..- ----	aircraft
Yugun	ware	ワレ	wa re	-.- ---	our troops
Teki	teki	テキ	te ki	.-.-- -.-..	enemy
Uyokutai	uyo	ウヨ	u yo	..- --	right wing
Chuotai	chiwo	チヲ	chi wo	..-. .---	center
sayokutai	sayo	サヨ	sa yo	-.-.- --	left wing
Yobitai	yohi	ヨヒ	yo hi	-- --..-	reserves
Daiissen	ise	イセ	i se	.- .---.	first line
Zenei	see	セエ	se e	.---. -.---	advance guard
Koei	koe	コエ	ko e	---- -.---	rear guard
Hontai	hon	ホン	ho n	-.. .-.-.	main body
Zenpei	sen	セン	se n	.---. .-.-.	vanguard
Kohei	kou	コウ	ko u	---- ..-	rear party
Sento	seto	セト	se to	.---. ..-..	head
Kobi	kohi	コヒ	ko hi	---- --..-	extreme rear
Shomen	men	メン	me n	-...- .-.-.	front (in meters)
Jucho	chiyo	チヨ シヨ	chi yo shi yo	..-. -- --.-. --	depth (in meters)
Shuryoku	shiyu	シユ	shi yu	--.-. -..--	main force
Ichibu	ichi	イチ	i chi	.- ..-.	part, partial
Shugo	shiu	シウ	shi u	--.-. ..-	assembly, concentration

Full Expression	Abbreviation	Katakana	Equivalent	Code		Translation
Tenkai	ten	テン	te n	·–·––	·–·–·	deployment
Zenshin	susu	スス	su su	–––·–	–––·–	advance
Teishi	toma	トマ	to ma	··–··	–··–	halt
Taikyaku	hiku	ヒク	hi ku	––··–	···–	retreat
Jinchisenryo	chin	チン	chi n	··–·	·–·–·	occupation of a position
Naru	naru	ナル	na ru	·–·	–·––·	preparations for attack completed
Naranai	nara	ナラ	na ra	·–·	···	preparations for attack not complete
Yuku	yuku	ユク	yu ku	–··––	···–	attack making progress
Yuri	yuri	ユリ	yu ri	–··––	––·	fighting developing favorably
Totsugeki	totsu	トツ	to tsu	··–··	·––·	charge
Tsuigeki	tsui	ツイ	tsu i	·––·	·–	pursuit making progress
Furi	furi	フリ	fu ri	––··	––·	situation unfavorable
Soshi	soshi	ソシ	so shi	–––·	––·–·	have been checked
Toppa	toha	トハ	to ha	··–··	–···	break through (at,...)
Horu	horu	ホル	ho ru	–··	–·––·	field work is continuing
Kuru ya	kiya	キヤ	ki ya	–·–··	·––	....(locality) appears to be preparing for attack
Teisatsu	tei	テイ	te i	·–·––	·–	state of ....(locality) and....(unit) is to be investigated and reported upon
Meirei	mei	メイ	me i	–···–	·–	issue orders to...(unit)

Full Expression	Abbrevi-ation	Kata-kana	Equiva-lent	Code		Translation
Sampeigo	san	サン	sa n	–·–·–	·–·–·	fire trench
Hoheijinchi	hochi	ホチ	ho chi	–··	··–·	artillery positions
Tetsujomo	tetsu	テツ	te tsu	·–·––	·––·	barbed-wire entangle-ments
Hikojo	hara	ハラ	ha ra	–···–	···	airdrome
Higashi	hika	ヒカ	hi ka	––··	·–··	east of....(locality)
Nishi	nishi	ニシ	ni shi	–·–·	––·–·	west of....(locality)
Minami	mina	ミナ	mi na	··–·–	·–·	south of....(locality)
Kita	kita	キタ	ki ta	–·–··	–·	north of....(locality)
Mae	mae	マエ	ma e	–··–	–·–––	in front of....(locality)
Ato	ato	アト	a to	––·––	··–··	behind....(locality)
Muko	kau	カウ	ka u	·–··	··–	towards....(locality)
Wataru	wata	ワタ	wa ta	–·–	–·	from.... to....
Migi	miki	ミキ	mi ki	··–·–	–·–··	right
Hidari	hita	ヒタ	hi ta	––··–	–·	left
Gozen	ze	ゼ	ze	·–––·	··	a.m.
Gogo	go	ゴ	go	––––	··	p.m.

NOTES ON OPERATIONS IN MALAYA

Tactical and Technical Trends, No. 15, December 31, 1942.

"One of the reasons for our failure in the Malayan Campaign was that we were mentally and physically surprised by actual conditions of jungle fighting." After arriving at this conclusion, British General Headquarters in India issued a long report containing an analysis of the difficulties faced by the British troops in Malaya, suggestions for overcoming them in future campaigns, and, finally, suggestions for specialized training of troops to fight in the jungle.

In this campaign, as in others, bombs and machine-gun fire from enemy aircraft had an unduly detrimental effect on the morale of the troops unless they were allowed to engage them with small-arms fire. The material effect of such firing is relatively unimportant compared with the morale effect, which is enormous.

The jungle growth in Malaya falls into two categories: primary jungle, which is natural vegetation that has not been touched; and secondary jungle, which consists of terrain cleared of primary jungle but subsequently overgrown by very dense underbrush. In the first type, visibility is usually from 20 to 30 yards, and on the tops of hills the foliage is quite thin. Travel through this type of vegetation is not too difficult and requires only a small amount of cutting. Secondary jungle, on the other hand, requires heavy labor to cut through the ferns and brambles; it is found on the sides of roads and the banks of rivers, often giving the impression that the primary jungle beyond it is also impassable.

In Malaya, as in nearly all jungle country, there are a small number of open areas, in this case, the tin mines. However, little use could be made of the effective fields of fire, since these areas were nearly always outflanked.

The British comments emphasize a striking similarity between jungle warfare and night operations, in that both favor the offensive. The extremely limited visibility, the small fields of fire, and the impossibility of securing effective artillery support all hinder the defenders and favor the attackers.

A. DIFFICULTIES OF JUNGLE WARFARE

One of the most significant features of jungle fighting was found to be the unusual amount of fatigue which troops felt in this type of warfare. Called upon to march long distances without the aid of their motor transport, often isolated from supplies and support, and subjected to the enervating climate and difficult terrain of the jungle, soldiers were much more susceptible to fatigue than usual.

Morale, too, was affected by conditions not encountered in normal types of warfare. Tactical situations often appeared much worse than they were, since control of subordinate units was frequently lost in the dense jungle where communications presented unusual difficulties. It was found that rumors were even more prevalent than usual among groups of soldiers, and this, also, was at least partially due to difficulties with communications. The British believe that greater efforts must be made to maintain communications, not only for command purposes but also to support morale, by keeping all the small groups informed of the local, and so far as possible, the general situation.

B. JAPANESE OFFENSIVE TACTICS

The Japanese invariably advanced on as broad a front as possible, making use of all available communications (roads, railways, rivers, and the sea) as well as sending their infantry through the jungle. In attacking, they would nearly always undertake to contain the forward defenses and then make an envelopment. The British stated that nearly every time that light holding attacks were made against their forward positions, they could be sure of an impending encirclement. It was also noted, however, that when the British flanks were effectively secured, the Japanese did not hesitate to make a frontal attack aimed at infiltration and penetration. Such tactics obviously emphasize the necessity for allotting the minimum number of troops to the strategic defense of vital areas and retaining the maximum number for counterattack. They also emphasize the vital necessity of maintaining control of these reserves through proper communications.

It is interesting to note that the Japanese ordinarily launch two encircling attacks in depth, the first to a depth of 1,000 yards, and the second to a depth of about 5 miles. These figures apply to a Japanese regiment. Ordinarily, when contact was made at about 0800, the first encircling attack came almost immediately and the second sometime in the early afternoon. The first, shallow attack was not considered dangerous by the British and in some actions the Japanese omitted this preliminary and concentrated on the larger encirclement. During these attacks, the Japanese employed a holding detachment against the British front lines.

C. ARTILLERY

The jungle did much to limit the effectiveness of artillery, but where it could be employed it caused the Japanese a great deal of trouble. Captured reports nearly always referred to British artillery in terms of the greatest respect. The best type of artillery fire was found to be a rolling barrage laid astride a road on a front of 300 to 400 yards.

D. TANKS

Since the few tanks that were used were confined to the roads, the problems of antitank units were greatly reduced. Often as many as 30 to 50 tanks participated in one attack, but they were usually easily ambushed. Although the fronts were not vulnerable to the 2-pounder, they could nearly always be knocked out by a hit on the side or the rear.

E. COMMUNICATIONS

Individual runners were the most satisfactory. Visual signal devices were practically useless, and there was seldom time or material to lay wire. Some use was made, however, of civilian communication facilities. When this was done, the exchanges had to be carefully guarded and supervised by military personnel, since the local operators could not be depended upon. In the few cases where wire was laid, it functioned satisfactorily, and was not so vulnerable to enemy bombing and artillery fire as it would have been in more open terrain. The range of radio was greatly reduced by the jungle, and it seldom worked at night. Small "walkie-talkies" were the most valuable form of radio and lent themselves particularly well to the operations of small groups. Code was almost never used below division headquarters, for runners took less time than coding and decoding.

F. PERSONNEL VEHICLES

Tracked carriers and armored cars were effectively used where the road net was satisfactory. The carriers, however, in addition to being vulnerable to armor-piercing ammunition, were also inviting targets for grenades dropped from trees, a favorite Japanese trick. Wire netting over the tops of carriers would have been an effective method of neutralizing this danger. The light machine gun on the carriers had the advantage of height and was almost never removed and used on the ground. The armored car, although even more road-bound than the tracked carrier, had the advantage of operating silently and could, therefore, be used in mobile surprise attacks. It also had heavier and better armor, making it less vulnerable than the carrier. In the withdrawal these armored cars were usually the last to go, for they were particularly suited for ambushing the enemy.

G. BRITISH SUGGESTIONS FOR OFFENSIVE TACTICS

In jungle warfare the advantages accruing to the attackers are so great that the British believe the careful working out of a tactical plan should be subordinated to seizing and maintaining the initiative. This does not mean that thorough grounding in tactics and techniques of small groups, and of the individual soldier should be minimized, but rather that "the essence of the encounter battle (meeting engagement) is that it must be fought automatically by all officers and men according to a battle procedure... constantly practiced and applied to all types of ground."

As a result of these observations this report suggested the following tactics to British troops:

The success of the encircling attack lies in its speed. To attempt this, highly trained jungle troops, capable of quick cross-country movement and well-trained in map reading, are employed to seize a part of the road from the enemy. This initial seizure is simply to establish control before the beginning of the main attack, which will be made against the rear of the enemy defenses. This main attacking force may be divided into 3 detachments: (a) the initial striking force which secures a strip of road (not more than 400 to 600 yards should be necessary for a battalion attack); (b) a second force which attacks the enemy's rear immediately upon seizure of the road; (c) a reserve which may be used either to exploit the action of the second force or to relieve the first if the latter has lost too heavily in its initial encounter.

The success of such an attack is dependent primarily upon supplies and speed, for there can rarely be assistance from supporting arms. Consequently, the point selected for the attack in the enemy's rear should provide good cover for the unsupported infantry.

In the jungle the frontal attack is normally made on a narrow front, astride a road. It is designed to exploit the fact that all control is concentrated along the road, and is executed with a relatively narrow artillery barrage, usually extending about 200 yards on either side of the road. One of its advantages is that it allows for greater use of artillery. The use of tanks will be effective only if the enemy is insufficiently supplied with antitank guns, and if the attacking infantry follows very closely behind the tanks.

To achieve the best results the British believe that this attack should be combined with infiltration on the flanks of the main attack. These infiltrating detachments should he given objectives well to the enemy's rear, such as bridges or ammunition dumps.

H. DEFENSIVE TACTICS

The defense, as stated, is inevitably hampered in jungle warfare. In the face of greatly superior enemy forces, when it is not possible to seize the initiative at once, the object must be a system of defense which will kill the maximum number of the enemy, but above all which will maintain the defending forces as a unit. Only by maintaining control is there any hope of reducing the enemy's numbers to the point where a counterattack can be launched. The static defense is as worthless in the jungle as in the desert, and the British now believe, for example, that the only way to hold a position for a prearranged number of days is to meet the enemy sufficiently far forward so that the delaying actions will last for the number of days desired. To apply these tactics requires troops of the highest caliber, for their morale will inevitably suffer in a series of even short withdrawals, and the tendency will be for smaller units to withdraw before they are ordered to do so.

Since control of the roads is the objective of both the forces, defense must take the form of a series of zones of resistance located in depth down the road. In successful defensive action in Malaya, battalion depth was about 2 miles and regimental depth up to 6 miles. Above all, the enemy must not be allowed to get completely in the rear of the defensive positions. Company defense areas are about 300 yards in diameter; and within platoons, squad defense areas should be about 100 yards apart. Squads themselves are usually dispersed in 2 or 3 groups, 30 yards from one another.

In order to conduct a defense successfully, normal Japanese tactics must be studied. The Japanese usually make initial contact on a road, with the objective of finding and containing the front line troops, as a preliminary to encirclement. Since this initial contact is made with considerable speed and at the expense of ordinary security measures, their leading formations are particularly vulnerable to ambush. A normal Japanese leading detachment would consist principally of a group of 4 or 5 bicyclists, followed at several hundred yards by another group of 60 or more bicyclists. After the forward group is allowed to pass, a successfully camouflaged ambush should be able to wipe out the large group following. Another type of ambush for these forward Japanese troops might consist of placing fairly strong, well-camouflaged forces on the flanks of a road, some distance in front of the other friendly positions. The Japanese are allowed to make contact, and to bring up their troops for the holding attack and subsequent encirclement; they may then be struck from the rear by the forward troops on the flank.

I. COUNTERATTACKS

The Malaya fighting indicated that in the jungle immediate rather than deliberate counterattacks were required. Counterattacks were invariably unsuccessful when ordered by higher command since the situation had nearly always changed, usually for the worse, by the time the attack was launched. On the other hand, immediate counterattacks by reserves of forward units were nearly always successful. One general type of counterattack proposed for the future is as follows:

When the enemy makes contact, the leading defending battalion immediately withdraws. The enemy is then allowed to push forward to a bridge, village, or other vital feature. At this point a surprise frontal attack is made. This method has the advantage of not breaking up the main body to place counterattacking units on a flank.

J. PATROLS

The British believe that in the jungle, fighting patrols, rather than mere observation patrols are always desirable. Patrols should aim to kill as many of the enemy as possible, giving information to their commander by "reporting by fire." This is based on the belief that events move so quickly in the jungle that a patrol which waits to report enemy movements on its return will invariably be giving stale and incorrect information. Patrols should also be considered as one of the best means of locating and disorganizing enemy encirclements during the approach march. Finally, the British believed that only small patrols can achieve the requisite mobility, and they recommend a patrol of one leader and two others.

SELECTIONS FROM JAPANESE FIELD INSTRUCTIONS

Tactical and Technical Trends, No. 16, January 14, 1943.

The task of interpreting Japanese tactics is considerably facilitated by a study of their own documents. The following extracts taken from translations of Japanese field instructions contain many concrete admonitions as to the action of small units in combat conditions.

*   *   *   *

A. MORALE

The unit commander himself must not give up hope or make pessimistic statements. In a battle always remember the "4 to 6 ratio" - if 4 of our men are knocked out, consider that we have got 6 of the enemy. Whatever may be our own losses, keep up morale. The more violent the fighting, the calmer and firmer must be the commander's bearing, orders, and words of command. It is also important, for the encouragement of morale, not to let the personnel of the unit know the number of killed and wounded, or their names.

In operations when our positions face those of the enemy, the most unpleasant thing is to see the tendency of our own personnel to fall into a passive attitude. This is the reaction of ambitious men who say "getting killed in our own positions is the same as being slaughtered without resistance. Our father and brothers are going to be ashamed of us. If I am going to be killed, I want to die fighting"—so this attitude is not to be construed as the result of cowardice. Although it may be a difficult task, the men must be made to feel that they are on the offensive, even when they are in a defensive position. For this purpose, it is necessary to carry out fierce counterattacks from time to time. With us, the fiercer the fighting, the higher our morale.

Heavy enemy shelling greatly affects morale, and sometimes troops will not fight as they should. The effect is still more marked when it results in casualties. Unit commanders must strive to stimulate morale, and be careful of their own actions and attitude. (At such times the men always watch the expression on the commander's face.)

To eradicate the sense of fear in raw soldiers, killings with the bayonet should be carried out whenever an opportunity occurs. Raw troops, being unused to fighting, suffer relatively heavy casualties, and attention should be paid to this point.

Before going into action, succession of command must always be clearly indicated. Unless this succession is defined right down to the last soldier, and training carried out until this becomes practically automatic, fighting may become confused if the unit commander becomes a casualty. When the unit commander is killed or wounded, the effect on the personnel is extremely great, and morale tends to decline. On the other hand, even if one man after another is killed, and the situation is tragic, if the men see their commander's face full of vigor, their courage increases a hundred-fold.

"After victory, tighten your helmet strings" says an old Japanese proverb. After fierce fighting, or during a pause in the battle, the mind is apt to relax. This is the most dangerous moment. Even men who are daring and determined during a charge, have a tendency to be cowardly as soon as the fighting changes to mopping-up operations, and only scattered fire and small numbers of enemy troops are encountered.

B. EXPENDITURE OF PERSONNEL

As a landing party staff officer says in his "Instruction in

Practical Strategy": "Would you throw away the lives of your men, who have been given into your keeping by the Emperor, by recklessly sending them on a frontal charge in the face of the enemy fire, ignoring your own shortcomings in leadership and strategy?" As a commander, bear this well in mind. In a word, your objective must be to attain the greatest results with the smallest sacrifice. If you order your men to advance, they will obey you in any circumstances and at all times. But remember that before doing this, you are to take the minutest precautions. Do not forget to explain to your men, as carefully as if they were little children, how and in what direction to advance, the places to watch, and what to do when shelled or attacked by hand grenades. For example, how many men would have come through unscathed if they had been ordered to lie down—"to get down until your head is on the ground." This may sound like a graceless criticism of men who have given their lives, but we believe many men have become casualties through their own carelessness and want of caution. It is true we have dedicated our lives to the Nation and will not begrudge them at any time, but we want to accomplish something by our death, and not to die uselessly. We want to die gloriously. We hope for a death worthy of a Samurai, like Lieutenant X, and we owe it to the men under our command to enable them to do likewise. If you do this, as the commanders of a unit you will have a measure of peace of mind.

Too much eagerness to do something outstanding must be strictly avoided; it has sometimes led to heavy losses. This is particularly true of units going into action for the first time. Some young soldiers think it heroic to expose themselves to the enemy; take care of this, particularly in a battle of positions.

Too long a wait in the same area will result in drawing concentrated fire from the enemy, and is inadvisable. When moving, the proportion of hits from bullets is smaller than when halted. In a charge, if you meet concentrated fire from the enemy at close quarters and lie down and stay glued to the same spot, you cannot advance. Also, the longer you halt, the more your will to advance is blunted, and the greater your casualties. Therefore, charges must be made with determination and daring. In this way, your casualties will be smaller, and your morale will be improved. If you act with determination, even the Gods will ward off harm, and in the midst of death there will be life. [Translator's note - Nothing really devotional about this - more a figure of speech than anything else.] A daring and determined attack is the key to victory.

C. MACHINE-GUN UNITS

In a naval landing party, there is practically no necessity for a machine-gun company. It is preferable to include in each company a machine-gun platoon under the command of the rifle company commander. From the nature of a naval landing party, there is practically no occasion on which a machine-gun company joins in the action as an independent unit with its machine guns. As a rule each platoon is detached, and is organized under the rifle unit company commander. This is particularly true in the case of street-fighting and fighting at close quarters. Even if a machine-gun company were independent, it would find it difficult to put up a vigorous fight without the support of the rifle units. Nowadays section training is the main consideration in machine-gun training, and the need for company exercises is not particularly felt.

All machine-gun personnel with the exception of the gunner must be armed with rifles. This is particularly necessary in street-fighting, fighting at close quarters, etc. Even when attacking and advancing, the carrying of rifles never impedes the advance. In case of an enemy attack, it is easy to make a sortie with the machine-gun ammunition personnel. The ideal rifle for machine-gun personnel is the short barrel rifle.

The loopholes of a machine-gun position must always be screened with pieces of cloth or matting. If the enemy can see through them, his snipers may fire at them, or he may concentrate his fire on them. This is particularly necessary in the case of apertures for heavy machine guns, which must be large on account of the angle of fire.

If two machine guns are used, they can be fired alternately, giving the enemy no pause for a counterattack, while the rifle units at the flanks must endeavor to create an opportunity for an attack. If is absolutely necessary to carry one shovel for each machine gun. If possible, four bags for sand should be carried for each gun.

The normal machine-gun squad should be increased by one man, and three boxes of ammunition should always be carried. Particularly in an advancing attack, there are occasions when replenishments from the rear do not arrive in time.

D. SNIPING

When the enemy takes to fortified trenches to try to stop our advances, the greatest precautions must be taken against sniping. The enemy usually waits for an interruption in our fire to send a single deadly shot.

When confronting the enemy, do not put your head out for reconnaissance or observation more than once from the same place. A sniper will have his rifle sighted to get you the second time. There are times when you suffer through underrating the enemy.

When fighting is protracted, there is a tendency to get accustomed to the enemy, and relax vigilance against enemy fire and hidden enemies. We have been sniped time and again. Pay particular attention to this.

E. EQUIPMENT

The fireman's hatchet is necessary for emergency engineering work in street fighting. An ax is a little too big. The fireman's hatchet is best when confronted by an enemy at close quarters.

Canteens should be kept filled to capacity at every opportunity. Those who carry only a small quantity of water, claiming that heavy equipment impedes their movements, are always those that try to drink from other men's canteens later. Bear in mind also that when men go into action for the first time they feel particularly thirsty.

F. ATTACKS

The best time to halt an advancing attack is about 1500. If the attack is not halted until after dusk, there is danger of our defense against enemy attacks relaxing; besides, our fighting efficiency next day is bound to deteriorate. When an advancing attack is halted, we must immediately build a satisfactory offensive position and not leave anything undone that we may be sorry for when the enemy attacks.

When an area is captured, mopping-up operations should be carried out as quickly as possible, and our gains consolidated. Abandoned enemy corpses must be given the coup de grace.

In a charge, the platoon commander must be at the head, as indicated in the Manual. The charge is the moment when hardship and fatigue reach their climax, from the commander of the unit down to the last man. At this time, if everyone is determined to carry out the unit commander's orders without hesitation, and if the platoon commander advances at the head of his men, the spirit of daring and solidarity aroused in the company will enable them to penetrate the enemy position.

G. MISCELLANEOUS

In maneuvers, we have always had it emphasized that we must know the tactical situation. During the battle of X a certain unit commander boasted that he had decided to make a charge and thereby greatly embarrassed his company commanders. We believe this was a case of blind decision. We had been ordered by the battalion commander to strengthen our position and defend it to the death - this means if your arms are broken, kick the enemy; if your legs are injured, bite him; if your teeth break, glare him to death. This spirit is expressed in the words "defense to the death." The time to launch a charge is when the enemy has reached the limit of exhaustion. In defense, we believe that if you can hang on to a position with one light machine gun, one platoon can successfully crush the enemy.

When wounded, the unit commander's permission must be obtained before leaving the firing line. If the unit commander is not in the vicinity, request should be made to another officer, or to an NCO of the section. This is clearly indicated in the Manual, and even if a man is ignorant of the regulation, common sense should tell him that this procedure should be followed. Sometimes a man leaves the firing line when his injuries are not such as to prevent him from continuing the fight. This is a most cowardly action.

No firing must be done at night. This is something we feel very keenly in the present fighting. Care must be taken in this respect, since it is the natural tendency when shot at, to shoot back. If we are maneuvered into firing by the enemy, we reveal our firing line, show him the position of our automatic weapons, and give him an outline on which he can base his tactics.

The enemy's camouflage is truly efficient. We have found it hard to discover him, and thereby have suffered unexpected losses. At over 500 yards, his camouflage cannot be distinguished, and great care must be taken. Training against camouflage should also be carried out.

The quickest means of communication after a battalion has deployed (with the exception of special orders) is by flag signalling if the visibility of the terrain permits. It is very important, therefore, for the commander of the unit headquarters not only to pay attention to the enemy, but also to keep in mind liaison with the commanders at the rear and flanks. It sometimes happens that when the fighting becomes particularly violent, the situation of every officer and man becomes absorbed by the enemy in front, and liaison with the commander has been temporarily cut off. Furthermore, where the terrain allows visibility, simple orders can be communicated much more quickly by flag signalling than if a number of runners are used over terrain full of "freaks," etc. Therefore, every member of a landing party should be proficient in sending and receiving flag signals.

TACTICS ON GUADALCANAL AND NEW GUINEA

Tactical and Technical Trends, No. 17, January 28, 1943.

The following notes on Japanese tactics were made after observation of fighting on Guadalcanal.

* * * *

The Japanese is a night fighter. He does not move or attack in the daylight, or even in moonlight. He waits till a dark night, moves in close, and attempts, by infiltration, to seep through a weak spot in the line. He then attempts to create confusion and thereby allow other Japanese troops to enter the line. Presumably, in case of a breakthrough, he would consolidate the next day, and prepare for another attack. In case of a rout, he would undoubtedly continue the attack in the daytime.

One method of attack used was for an advanced detail to move in quietly, followed by a larger detail making considerable noise. The noise of the large detail subsequently covered the cutting of wire, brush, etc., by the advanced detail and allowed it to break through the lines. When our troops heard the larger of the two details, they allowed them to approach to very close range before opening fire. However, by this time the smaller detail was in rear of our force and began to fire. Unless proper security measures are taken to give warning of this and similar tricks, the effect of the fire from the rear is apt to be so demoralizing as to cause troops to break.

Defense against Japanese attacks must principally be against infiltration. It is obviously impossible for defense lines to be manned with a man every 2 feet, and even though it were possible to have the men this close together, some Japanese would still seep through. A defense should be organized with strongpoints properly adapted to terrain features. If possible they should be organized for all-around defense, with barbed wire and land mines in front of positions, and wire behind. Intervals between strongpoints must, of course, be covered with strong automatic and mortar fire, and if the intervals are large enough, with artillery fire. Reserve elements should be employed to wipe out the isolated enemy elements that break through.

Several bands of barbed wire should be laid around a position, and for this use concertina wire is preferable to the double apron, as it is much harder to cut. Troops expecting to defend in jungle terrain should carry large amounts of concertina wire. It is suggested that several tin cans or other noise-making devices be strung along this wire so as to betray the general direction of attack.

The Japanese use very few commands in battle. Apparently the troops are thoroughly drilled in the particular operation and continue through with it. Very pistols, somewhat similar to ours, are used to show the direction of advance. In the attacks against us, a red Very pistol light was used, and served the purpose of converging all units in that particular vicinity toward a certain direction. This, when discovered, enabled us to move reserves to the threatened area. A green Very light meant a withdrawal. If Japanese signal lights can be captured and used, it would undoubtedly be possible to create confusion in their lines by shooting off flares at the wrong time. Our own Very pistol flare differed enough from the Japanese light so that it did not fool them.

Quite a number of the Japanese, probably officers, speak perfect English and use this to trick our troops. On one occasion a Japanese was heard to call out, "Hold your fire, we are American troops. I am bringing in a patrol." Upon several occasions our telephone wires were tapped, and attempts made to get the operator to divulge information. In using the telephone, some type of authenticator must be used, and even then no information of value should be transmitted over the phone. The same applies to radio transmission.

The Japanese are not good shots. Over a hundred yards "they can't hit the well-known bull with a bass fiddle." They have plenty of machine guns, both light and heavy, but are unable to use them to the best advantage. They almost always fire in one direction, and very seldom traverse. Their clips hold 30 rounds, and the gunner generally fires the entire clip without stopping.

The Japanese we encountered were long on guts and short on judgment. They charged time and again against machine guns and 37-mm guns loaded with canister. They seemed unable to change a plan once decided upon and attempted to carry it out even though it was apparently impossible. This is no doubt due, to some extent, to the impossibility of getting the changes around in a night battle. If beaten, and he must be badly beaten before he is stopped, he withdraws to some predetermined bivouac area to "lick his wounds," reorganize, and prepare a new plan. Aggressive patrolling should be conducted the day following an attack in order to drive his patrols away from our positions. Strafing and personnel bombing should be used as much as possible, as well as artillery concentrations.

Grenades are used extensively by the enemy. The Japanese grenade can be used either as a rifle or as a hand grenade. Strictly speaking, it is not used as a rifle grenade but is fired from a grenade thrower.

The training of troops likely to fight the Japanese should be at least three-quarters at night — night marches, night attacks, organizing defense at night, etc. Each individual must be trained so that no matter what the situation may be, he will not become panic-stricken, but continue to fight. There will be times when bodies of troops will become separated, but they must continue their effort and not try to withdraw. Each individual must understand every detail concerning the operations.

* * * *

A high-ranking American staff officer who observed operations in New Guinea submits the following brief comments about what he saw of Japanese tactics and his opinions as to the measures designed to cope with such tactics.

"The Japanese have covered themselves defensively by a multitude of extremely well-constructed and camouflaged bunkers (or combination coconut tree trunks and earth pillboxes). Progress in advance can only be made by killing and/or 'digging out' the Japanese occupying each bunker—a slow, tedious and difficult process.... The operations have demonstrated one thing conclusively, and that is the need for more detailed, extended, and thorough training of the individual soldier and the squad, section, and platoon leaders. Scouting and patrolling, reconnaissance, and all phases of small unit leadership should be featured.... The individual should be trained in finding his way through thickly wooded and swampy areas and should be taught that such areas are an advantage to the offense instead of something to be looked on with concern and hesitation. The fear of swampy areas should be overcome by wading through them in training. Night field training should be the rule and daylight field operations the exception...."

JAPANESE ACTION AGAINST U.S. TANKS

Tactical and Technical Trends, No. 19, February 25, 1943.

As indicated in the previous article on antitank tactics used by the Russians, tanks must be supported by other arms. A series of incidents involving destruction or loss of American tanks in the Solomons is reported by a member of our armed forced. This report shows the importance, at least in close country, of closely supporting tanks with infantry.

On Guadalcanal a platoon of six light M-3 tanks was sent to aid the infantry forces fighting to the west of the Lunga River. Headquarters tank and tanks Nos. 1, 4, and 5 were moved forward in column to attack enemy machine guns on the edge of the jungle across a clearing from the infantry. Tank No. 4 went into the jungle and has not been found since. Tank No. 5, after entering a short way, backed out of the jungle without having found any targets. The driver of Tank No. 5 said that near the edge of the jungle, the Japanese threw grenades under the tracks. The explosion of the grenades would cause the tank to jump somewhat but did not cause any noticeable damage. This tank was stationary when it was hit on the right forward side of the turret. The shell penetrated the tank and hit the opposite turret wall where it exploded. The driver estimated that the antitank gun which hit his tanks was about 100 yards away. Filling from the shell ran down and began to burn with a yellow flame and bluish smoke. The driver stated that the fumes were sharp and stifling and caused the mouth to dry and pucker. Almost immediately after the first hit, a second hit was received in the right side of the turret. The shell penetrated and spattered filling around, which likewise began to burn on the floor and on the top of the ammunition lockers. Efforts to put out the fire were unavailing and the survivors jumped out of the tank and started for the rear. Japanese troops were moving toward the tank and shortly after it was abandoned, the driver saw it burning fiercely, but did not know whether the Japanese had thrown gasoline on it or not.

The Headquarters tank was disabled by a hit on the right sprocket wheel while about forty feet into the jungle.

Tank No. 1 was circling in the open field in rear of Tank No. 5 when it was hit in the turret. The lieutenant and radioman were killed but the tank was recovered. Fire in Tank No. 1 was extinguished without great difficulty. The diameter of the hole in Tank No. 1 was slightly larger than that of our 37-mm shell.

The company commander estimated that from the number of hits received by his tanks, and the location of the tanks when hit, the enemy had five antitank guns. The caliber of the enemy guns was believed to be 47-mm.

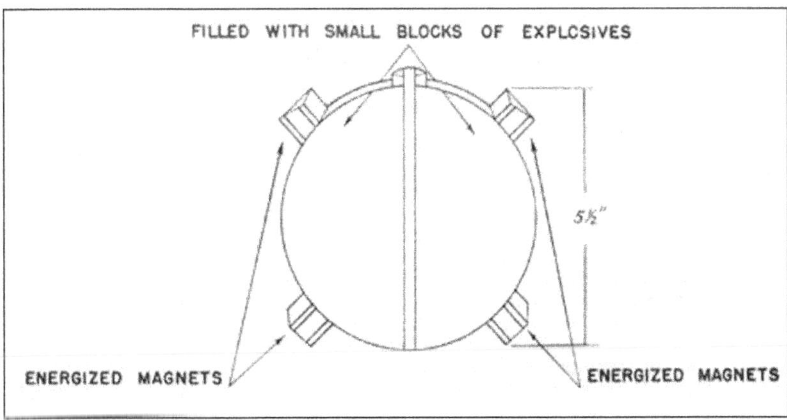

Comment: This is the first (at time reported) encounter with the Japanese 47-mm antitank gun. It easily penetrated turret armor of light M-3 tanks. The action of the shell after entering the tank seems to indicate an explosive filler made from a picrate derivative. The enemy apparently waited for a close range shot before opening fire.

There was no evidence of the use of the magnetic tank grenade although some had been captured previously on Guadalcanal (see sketch).

Mutual support between tanks and infantry in close terrain is still a necessity.

REGULATIONS GOVERNING JAPANESE TROOPS OCCUPYING CONQUERED AREAS

Tactical and Technical Trends, No. 20, March 11, 1943.

Having consolidated their earlier gains of the war in the Southwest Pacific area, the Japanese began to advance to the south and to the east in the spring of 1942. The push southward has been marked by the Battle of the Coral Sea, the Japanese occupation and loss of Guadalcanal, and the fighting in southeastern New Guinea. Such operations involved not only the capture of the land areas concerned, but also their administration and defense so that they might be available as bases for future operations. Troops were specially detailed to follow the initial attack or advance and take over the administration and defense of the captured areas. They might be referred to as occupation or base troops.

Such elements undoubtedly moved south to the large Japanese advance base at Rabaul, New Britain, in the spring of 1942, as part of a major operation intended to culminate in an attack on Australia. By May 1942 Japanese troops had landed on Tulagi near Guadalcanal, and by the middle of July work had been begun on Henderson Field on Guadalcanal. On July 1, 1942 the Japanese "8th Base Force" was at Rabaul, though elements thereof had already probably moved south. There follows a translation of a Japanese document dealing with the duties of the "Guard Forces," i.e., the troops detailed to the administration and defense of captured areas.

* * * *

EIGHTH BASE FORCE - REGULATIONS NO. 3

JULY 1, 1942 (RABAUL)

DUTIES OF THE GUARD FORCES

a. General Principles

(1) The areas to be defended by these forces include the land, sea, and air in the regions occupied by the Imperial Forces southeast of the equator to New Guinea and to the east thereof.

At the important points within the wide areas which these units will control, bases will be established from which to advance the plans for attacking the east coast of Australia, in conjunction with other friendly forces. These units will also guard the conquered areas, preserve the peace, and protect the sea lanes. A most important duty will be to enforce military rule in conquered areas.

The areas which these units are to defend, and from which advances will be made, is near the focal point of the concentrated strength of U.S., British, and Australian forces. Our units are to perfect the defenses of the important areas and then advance, intercepting the enemy, wrecking his combined operations, and annihilating him. This operation, we believe, is the key to the successful termination of the Greater East Asia War.

(2) All men of these units should consider the above-mentioned duties as being of foremost importance; and they must fight daringly in the front lines of this, the most important battleground beneath the southern stars, overcoming all difficulties and breaking down all barriers, concentrating all efforts and striving always at fever pitch for Japan—vowing to win this great battle.

However, that enemy sea, land, and air attacks will become vigorous and persistent, is something that we naturally expect from a standpoint of strategy. For this reason, take proper security measures in all defensive patrols and in an emergency be ready to launch immediately a full-scale counterattack. While bearing in mind that defensive measures may have to be taken, always retain the initiative and make it your number-one duty to overpower the enemy. The various units which are assigned to the defense of important points will desperately defend their allotted areas, and will also concentrate their efforts on keeping to a minimum the damage caused by enemy attacks.

(3) Discipline is the core of a military force, and naturally, in times of battle, all duties will be performed in a soldierly manner. The noble ideals of loyalty and patriotism are naturally related to leadership and obedience, and these are the basis for the fighting strength so manifest in the Imperial Forces. This is brought about by harmony and order within the unit itself. The soldier, showing his love for the soul and spirit of Japan, adds luster to his unit, and if this spirit be shown by one who has undergone hardships, then he gives greater glory to the Imperial Forces.

Front-line duty involves many factors which make it different from peacetime duty on board a warship or within a unit. At the present time, in the Imperial Forces, this is evident in stricter discipline and a flourishing martial spirit. The importance of these factors must never be overlooked.

If you think that due to a hasty expedition to foreign parts, or because of special circumstances occurring once in ten thousand times, there is any exception to this rule of strict discipline, you are under a great illusion. All commanders must make this matter their first concern and never relax their vigilance, being always ready to guide their men along the right path.

(4) If these units obey and follow their duty as outlined above, their strategic mission in offensive and defensive actions and in the guarding of the sea lanes will be successfully accomplished. However, in places where no civil government has been established, this force will also, without neglecting its strategical duties, enforce order within the various areas

and assist in the civil administration. While one can say that a knowledge of how to govern foreign people is not easily come by, the indomitable, peerless Imperial Forces, who never violate a solemn and fearful discipline, will be able to work together with these people and rule. However, there should be a period in which the subordinate people should be led and trained.

b. General Functions

(1) Commands will be strictly carried out by these units, whether acting alone or in conjunction with other units.

When operations involving large forces and concentrated efforts are necessary in order to carry out the strategy within the areas in question, the methods to be adopted will depend on the orders of the commander-in-chief of the operations as a whole. In cases where remnants of the enemy within these areas are to be mopped up, or where the troops are to be used for the maintenance of order, these tasks will be carried out according to the plan of the guard-force or garrison-force commanders.

(2) The guard-force command will make the plans for the defense of the areas under its control, plan the distribution of manpower, guns, boats, and weapons, establish a system of defense, give the orders for carrying out a successful defense, and generally prepare for battle.

(3) The guard forces will, conditions permitting, carry out mopping-up operations within the area, particularly against enemy communication facilities. At the same time they will extend the zone of our influence.

(4) The guard forces will, taking into account local conditions, establish observation posts and communication centers, and send out patrols. Communications will be established as quickly as possible; this is one of the most important factors in a successful defense.

(5) Protection of sea-borne traffic depends largely on ships and planes, and will be under the control of the superior commander.

The guard-force commander and the garrison-force commanders will devote careful attention to the conditions of enemy and friendly sea lanes within their areas, and inform approaching friendly ships of these conditions. Also, the commanders will assist in guarding ships entering and leaving port, taking on or unloading cargo, and at anchor.

(6) In case friendly ships are present within their zone of command, the base forces and guard forces will, as the home force, assist the ships in carrying out their strategy, replenish supplies, and enable them to get some rest, etc. This is one of the most important points in carrying out the strategy of the Imperial Forces, and in manifesting their cooperation. The advancement of war strategy in this area depends largely on the work of the air force, and cooperation is therefore doubly important.

(7) In case there should be an airbase in the area, the air defense organization and patrol will be under the command of the air force; but the guarding of the area and the AA defense will be the duty of the guard force. Therefore, it is necessary to assist the air force in building up a speedy system of communications for patrol work.

(8) In case a friendly force under a different command stops in the area, it is necessary for the commanders to assure cooperation by reaching an understanding regarding any operations and by making clear the responsibilities of each.

(9) Keep the communication instruments always in a state of perfect preparation. In case they are not prepared, you must be ready to handle important communications swiftly and surely by such auxiliary means as flags, signal fires, and rockets.

In the case of reports and messages, you must not, by vainly concentrating on speed of delivery at the expense of essential accuracy, cause superior officers and friendly forces to err in their dispositions. Speed is to be sought after having prepared the important points of the message (for example, with regard to attack of enemy planes—the number of planes, types, direction of attack and withdrawal, results, damage, etc.), and having made the text simple and clear.

(10) It is the duty of the superior officers to see that guard forces in remote outlying districts get necessary reports and suitable supplies, medical care, etc. However, since there are many cases when it is not easy to do this on account of the conditions of communications and tactical situation, each unit must do its best to improvise as required, and each commander must advance of his own accord and strive to grasp the general situation.

c. Internal Duties

(1) The daily routine depends upon the orders of the superior commander, but there is nothing to prevent the guard-force commander from making changes in accordance with the military situation, the work being done, the weather, etc. In short, it is most essential to promote a bright, interesting, pleasant life in the field: on the one hand, by planning an appropriate daily routine, weekly routine, and work schedule, thus achieving the best and most efficient plan for every sort of situation; and, on the other hand, by appropriate training, rest, and recreation.

(2) Leisure time should be utilized to the fullest possible extent in ardent training which should be carried out realistically. Also, encourage proficiency in military arts and athletics. This is the best way to improve and refine the efficiency of the whole force, make it energetic, and promote discipline and morale. The commanding officer must always give thought to these matters and not neglect to put them into practice.

When activities against the enemy are comparatively simple, "spiritual laxity" may easily arise before you know it in the environment of the front lines. It exhibits itself first in careless dress and sloppy saluting; then, in not a few cases, discipline relaxes and fighting power is lowered, so attention is required on this point.

(3) In combat, and in everyday training and duty, it is most essential both for the display of the force's military strength and for the promotion of efficiency in every sort of work that the officers be among the ranks, leading and supervising. Because the effect of this is to form a crack unit in which officers and men are harmoniously united, it is traditionally a virtue of the Imperial Navy. In forces engaged in operations and in front-line duty, the officers must give attention to this point.

(4) In operations in the pestilential and torrid tropics, great care is necessary to avoid losses due to sickness, particularly the epidemic diseases peculiar to these regions. The points to which this force should pay attention in the various areas which it guards are as follows:

(a) Divide up the area occupied by the units, and the important places of the vicinity, and within these areas and, insofar as possible, outside of them, make it impossible for disease-carrying insects to appear or spread. (We refer you to the results obtained in the area at Rashun taken over by the navy after the invasion, where mosquitoes were virtually eliminated after 2 1/2 months and the sanitary situation greatly improved).

(b) Always get rid of waste water, and do not permit even a small amount of stagnant water to stand in empty tin cans.

(c) Always cut weeds short, and try to see that air circulates well through the trees.

(d) All garbage is to be transported to an established place at some distance and disposed of. Combustible matter is to be burnt every day.

(e) When there are damp areas with poor drainage in the vicinity, quickly devise means of draining them, and also cover them with waste oil.

(f) Men must sleep under mosquito netting.

(g) When moving about in the bush, be especially careful about your clothes (do not have your legs exposed, and if necessary use an anti-mosquito mask and gloves), and when resting or going to bed take strict precautions against mosquitoes.

(h) Follow strictly medical directions as to the taking of preventive medicines.

(5) The commanding officer of a remote guard force must take care to report to his superiors without delay the tactical situation, and also from time to time the general situation, health conditions, and other essential matters. Also, he must be alert to utilize boats and airplanes for the transmission of reports, orders, etc., to keep his force fully supplied, to maintain close liaison with his superior officers, and to prevent delays in the military preparations and ordinary duties of his own unit. In case of wounds or sudden illness in a force which has no doctor, the commanding officer is to get instructions quickly by message.

(6) Enemy property and captured goods must be properly disposed of in accordance with the various regulations. For this reason the commanding officer is to be conversant beforehand with the rules concerned. There is nothing to prevent the force from requisitioning and using whatever it needs from enemy produce, boats, houses, furniture, etc.; however, since the chief items, such as radio stations, power plants, etc., must be treated as national property from now on, you must report on their condition and strive to repair and preserve them.

(7) You should utilize spare time from duties to cultivate vegetables and fruit trees, and to raise chickens, pigs, etc., thus giving some ease and interest to your life and supplying some of your own provisions.

d. Treatment of Natives and Foreigners

(1) The natives of this area are in general simple and docile and tend to respect their masters. Each village is controlled autonomously under its chief (sometimes there is a main chief over the chiefs of a certain area or a number of villages), and if you can get the chiefs to direct the people favorably, it will make control comparatively easy and contribute a good deal of efficiency to labor conditions.

On the other hand, because of the past system of control, they have the habit of asserting their rights (they easily forget their duties), and many of them, having been affected by church education and being led by white missionaries, persist in those manners. The following points should be the general standard in leading and handling the natives:

(a) By the application of the authoritative and strict rules of the Imperial Army and by judicious direction, bring them to give us true respect and obedience. Induce them to become Japanese subjects. Make them realize that the Imperial Army will protect their lives and property, and that at the same time they must faithfully perform their duties.

(b) Prohibit the religious teaching (usually accompanied by schooling) which they have hitherto had from the white missionaries, but do not restrict the individual faith of the natives.

(c) Although you may make every effort to instill them with the Japanese type of spiritual training in its entirety, it will be hard for them to understand and usually there will be no results. For the present, make them understand well the great power and prestige of Japan and the superiority of the Japanese race, and bring them to trust us, admire us, and be devoted to us.

(d) Although the administration of justice is controlled by the civil government, the rendering of fair decisions in unimportant local matters will contribute to public order.

Be especially careful that there are none among them who through contacts with or induced by Europeans and Americans, give aid to the enemy. In such cases take severe measures, and when the offense is serious seek the direction of higher authority.

(e) Do not enter their dwellings nor chat with them on a level of equality.

(f) In view of the fact that they respect their women and have the custom of taking a fierce and daring revenge for offenses against them, never approach the native women.

(g) Since they respect property, always pay a proper price for things, and especially pay them properly when they have finished their work. In this matter follow the regulations of the civil government.

(h) Choose the chief carefully, respect and support his position as intermediary, and make him display his authority and ability in directing the people.

(i) Try to have labor and service carried out under the orders and direction of the chief; it is necessary that supervision be strict. Use experienced natives for the sanitary improvement set forth in paragraph 4 of part c above. Furthermore, in view of the fact that under the old regime, the natives used to work twice a week on the nearby roads under the direction of their chief and this was considered a duty, have them continue the custom.

(2) The Chinese are scattered about in the various areas to be controlled, living in small communities, and making use of their characteristic commercial talents to gain an economic foothold. In not a few cases they exploit the natives' labor. We may make use of the trades and business agencies of those who cooperate with us in good faith; however, in view of the actual situation in this area, where there are no remaining Japanese residents, the Chinese must not be permitted to extend excessively their

economic foothold.

(3) Enemy aliens who are hostile are naturally to be dealt with according to regulations. However, in the case of those who are not hostile and who honestly wish to cooperate with us, investigate them and seek the instructions of higher authority.

(4) The missionaries and Axis nationals (those remaining are mostly Germans) insist on being treated as priests and citizens of allied nations and, on the surface, promise to cooperate with us, but the real intention of many of them is to maintain their former rights, profits, and foothold, and to extend their businesses and try to prepare for the period after the war. Investigate them very strictly and, without being excessively high-handed on the surface, direct matters in such a way as to emasculate gradually their power, interests, enterprises, etc. If necessary, seek instructions from higher authority. Base your relations with, and treatment of these people on the following standard:

(a) Under the former regime the churches and their institutions were recognized as a form of the national government. As part of Imperial territory, their churches and their proselyting and education are now to be prohibited.

(b) Under the former government, with the exception of land belonging to the churches, private ownership of land was not recognized, and all enterprises relating to land were regulated by a lease granted for a definite period of time. For this reason the property and enterprises of the churches cannot be permitted to continue in their present status of vested interests. Of course, that which is already clearly private property is to be respected.

(c) At the beginning of this war, the Australian government rigorously selected from among the missionaries of Axis countries those who showed real sincerity in cooperating with Australia and who promised never to aid the enemies of Australia during the war; these were allowed to remain. At present there are quite a number of Germans and Italians who have been sent to Australia and detained there. Accordingly, there is a good deal of doubt about letting the present Axis missionaries simply go on exercising their special rights in our occupied areas, as "religionists" under international law.

(d) In case there is argument regarding the grounds and procedure in the above paragraphs, avoid entering deeply into vain discussions and seek instructions from higher authority.

e. Military Administration

The government of the occupied territories is in the hands of the Japanese civil administration, but, since the guard force must cooperate with and assist the civil authorities, we summarize here the essential points of the military administration policies of this force.

(1) Government

(a) This force will try to extend military administration over the occupied areas and to control them, quickly eliminating any hostile activity and restoring public order and discipline. Also, the force will devise means of self-support, and search for and secure important defense materials.

(b) Root out the white man's influence by the policy of controlling important points with the power of the Imperial Forces, and gradually extend the power of the administration over the whole area.

(c) Govern the natives, with the chiefs as the core of local autonomous government, under the direct guidance of the civil authority or a substitute organization. We may use carefully selected white men who cooperate with us and swear loyalty for this purpose.

(d) The churches and church-supported education of the old

regime is prohibited. Respect the religious faith, customs, and private property of the natives. Guide the masses of the people so as to make them gratefully contented with the prestige and authority of the Imperial Forces; make them return quickly to their occupations and cooperate actively with our policies.

(e) Always endeavor to mollify the masses with propaganda and to make them understand the meaning of our policies. Drive home the fact that it is natural that in war time the special demands of production, and the monetary and labor policies, should occasion heavy burdens to the people. Make them realize that behind the favors and the soothing propaganda is the might of the brave Imperial Forces, and that they have no other course than to rely on us and cooperate with us.

(f) Endeavor to restore and utilize the native constabulary system of the former government. Prohibit entirely the carrying of weapons by the natives.

(g) Restore the native public schools as quickly as possible, and give instruction with suitable persons as teachers. Furthermore, make propaganda capital out of giving the natives free medical service insofar as the exigencies of the war permit.

(2) Development of Industry and Expansion of Production

(a) For the present the first thing in the development of industry is to meet the requirements for the support of the force and of the various policies adopted, and at the same time to get as much as possible of the products of the land to help out the "Materials Movement Plan in Japan."[1]

(b) Do all you can to get the men and materials needed for development from local resources. Endeavor to use the

1 The Materials Movement Plan is evidently designed to effect the movement of raw materials, such as iron ore, petroleum, manganese, nickel ore, and bauxite, from the occupied areas to Japan.

labor of the natives, and try to make practical use of local facilities and materials.

(c) The land and all natural resources are government property, and, for the present, private ownership of them will not be recognized.

(d) The leasing, renting, and developing of government lands and resources will be permitted in the case of influential, trusted Japanese commercial firms. (All matters under this paragraph will be executed by the civil administration.) Permits granted in this area at present are as follows:
Nanyo Bocki Kaisha (South Seas Trading Company)
Nankyo Suisan Kaisha (Southern Development Marine Products Company)

(e) The expansion of production for the present will emphasize materials necessary to military operations and the production of provisions necessary for the support of the force. Otherwise, expansion will be managed according to the "Industrial Development and Production Expansion Plan,"[2] established by the civil government. Apart from the above, the securing and investigation of essential resources are in the hands of the civil government.

(3) Finance and Currency

(a) For the present, war notes[3] will be the currency.

(b) In view of the fact that financial and monetary problems will have a serious effect on the future government, everyone will follow the policies fixed by the civil administration and endeavor to be economical.

---

2 The Industrial Development and Production Expansion Plan is probably that part of Japan's economic policy which is concerned with obtaining the raw materials for the Materials Movement Plan, as well as rehabilitating and developing local industries to producing goods for local military needs.

3 Special currency issued in occupied areas.

JAPANESE FIELD WORKS AT BUNA

Tactical and Technical Trends, No. 21, March 25, 1943.

The taking of the Japanese positions in the Buna area (southeastern New Guinea) was a relatively lengthy process. Much of the difficulty was occasioned by the strong field works constructed by the enemy, and by the tenacity with which these works were held. Of interest, therefore, is the following extract from a report made by a U.S. Army engineer.

* * *

The enemy bunkers and dugouts in the Buna area were constructed of coconut-palm logs, dirt, sand, and sand bags, covered with natural camouflage. In some instances, pieces of armor plate were set up. No concrete positions were found. The log-and-dirt bunker construction was done carefully, and strongly. The corner posts were firmly embedded in the ground, and the horizontal logs neatly and strongly attached and interwoven. Several alternating layers of logs and earth were generally used to give full protection against mortars and light artillery. Roofs were thick and were also made of alternating layers, giving excellent protection. Bunkers were connected to systems of radiating fire and communication trenches on both sides. In some instances, underground trenches were used, and the enemy used these to place snipers in our midst even after they had long been driven from the general area. Leaves and grass were well used to camouflage all bunkers; in addition, the bunkers had been planned and built for just this purpose long before the campaign actually started, and the quick jungle growth, sprouting up over the earthworks, gave first-class natural camouflage.

The enemy work was generally neat and strong. One position in Buna Mission, consisting of kitchens, latrines, dugouts, and trenches, was, in consideration of the locale and the terrific bombardment that it had endured, a model of neatness and efficiency.

The enemy dugout positions were well sited and mutually supporting. It was extremely difficult, if not impossible, to bypass any of the positions, each of which had to be reduced in turn.

It would be impossible to overstress the tenacity with which the Japs clung to their prepared positions. Grenades, and ordinary gun and mortar fire were completely ineffective. There were many instances (not isolated ones) where dugouts were grenaded inside, covered with gasoline and burned, and then sealed with dirt and sand—only to yield, 2 or 3 days later, Japs who came out fighting. One souvenir hunter, entering, 4 days after the battle, a dugout that had been sealed, was chased out by a Japanese officer wielding a sword. Some of the instances in which Japs lived on in these positions, through the burning and the detonation, in the filth and gore, when sorely wounded themselves, are almost incredible.

JAPANESE RUSES—BUNA AREA

Tactical and Technical Trends, No. 21, March 25, 1943.

The extensive use of deception and ruses by the Japanese is well known. Below are described two which were used in the Buna area (Southeastern New Guinea).

A. "DUMMY" SNIPERS

An American patrol advancing up the coast was fired on by a sniper in a tree. They halted, located him, and apparently shot him down. They then advanced and were fired on again. This happened several times. Thorough investigation revealed that one sniper had been holding up the patrol, and dummies had been placed in other trees. After the Americans had fired sufficient shots, these dummies were dropped by a pulley arrangement. This caused the Americans to suppose that they had cleared the opposition.

In another case, the sniper's dummy was rigged so that it could be pulled back up into place; the sniper made the mistake of pulling it back up too soon, giving away his ruse.

B. "SHORT" ROUNDS

The morale and spirit of an Allied unit advancing under covering fire of friendly artillery was seriously affected by this ruse. Every time our guns opened up to provide covering fire for an advance, or fired on any target, the one known Jap 70-mm gun in the Government Gardens area also opened up and placed its rounds among our forward elements. The Japanese timed the activity of their own gun to coincide exactly with that of our supporting artillery. This made the troops imagine that they were being fired on by their own guns.

JAPANESE TACTICS ON GUADALCANAL

Tactical and Technical Trends, No. 21, March 25, 1943.

The following miscellaneous observations on Japanese tactics on Guadalcanal were made by a U.S. Marine colonel, commander of one of the Marine regiments.

* * * *

The Jap has been taught that he is invincible. He is accustomed to having the enemy run when Japanese elements get around their enemy's flanks and rear. He is also accustomed to the enemy running when he charges with the bayonet. In his night attacks, he expects the enemy to be caught in front of or on the tactical objective (always an identifiable terrain or other feature) and to be defeated; thus, the mission of his night operations is accomplished.

Consequently he has been upset, confused, and defeated by American troops who do not run, who themselves charge with the bayonet, and who are not where they are expected to be in night attacks—instead, they counterattack when the Japanese are confused and in process of reorganizing after having reached their night-attack objective.

In night attacks the Japanese would send advance parties by the valleys through the denser cover, reserving the more open terrain of the higher ground for the main body and main effort. They would have the main body make considerable noise in order to drown out any noise the advance parties might make. The Jap has had the advance parties clear away jungle growth along avenues of subsequent approach for larger units, and has “blazed” the trails thus cleared with luminous paint. The Jap moves his main forces up in closed-up columns—partly for reasons of command control.

For purposes of control and orientation, Japanese night attacks followed clearly defined terrain features, e.g., a crest ridge-line or a stream. The Japanese selected night-attack objectives from observation of our dispositions at sunset. If he later fails to find these dispositions where he expects them, he becomes confused in the dark and does not know where to look for us. It would take him an hour or two to get reorganized, and that was the time to counterattack him. Heavy casualties were inflicted on him then.

On Tulagi, the Jap took up his positions on the reverse slopes. This gave him better visibility up against the crests and sky, and permitted intense surprise fire of devastating effect at short ranges. However, when he counterattacked at night out of these positions, he suffered so many casualties that he did not have men enough to hold his reverse-slope positions the next day.

The Japanese machine-gun dugouts were held in strengths of 10 to 12 men. When one man was killed, another stepped up and manned the gun. This required every man to be killed, and so the positions held out for hours. Immediately after the Jap discovers a machine gun, he will send over mortar bombs, usually within 10 minutes. The Jap digs in wherever he stops. In a few minutes he will have a slit trench, and in 20 minutes a man-deep foxhole.

JAPANESE DATE SYSTEMS

Tactical and Technical Trends, No. 21, March 25, 1943.

It may be useful to recapitulate the systems now used by the Japanese in writing dates.

a. According to mythology, the Japanese Empire was founded in the year 660 B.C., and it is from this date that Japanese years are calculated in one system of writing dates. For example, our 1940 is the Japanese 2600, and so on. Type numbers for Japanese aircraft and various other military equipment are often derived from this system of dates. The last two digits of the year concerned, until and including 2599 (1939), are used for the type number; from 2600 (1940) onward, the last digit alone is used. Type "97" was adopted in the year 2597 (1937), Type "0" (zero) in 2600 (1940), Type "1" in 2601 (1941), and so on.[4]

b. In more general usage, however, is the practice (in use since 1868) of numbering years from the start of each Emperor's reign. A name is chosen for each reign, and a given year is referred to by the number of years that have elapsed since the reign started. The name of the reign of the present Emperor, which began in 1926, is Showa (Enlightened Peace); 1943 is thus the 18th year of Showa, or more simply "Showa 18."

c. The Western or Christian calendar is also in common use among the Japanese.

---

4 For the use of the term "Zero" as applied to aircraft, see Tactical and Technical Trends, No. 19, p. 1.

THREE JAPANESE INCENDIARIES

Tactical and Technical Trends, No. 22, April 8, 1943.

Aside from incendiary bombs, the Japanese are reported to have at least two types of incendiary grenades and at least one type of incendiary mortar shell. For general information on Axis incendiary munitions, see Tactical and Technical Trends, No. 14, p. 12.

A. HALF-KILOGRAM INCENDIARY GRENADE

This grenade, 50-mm in diameter, approximately 5.3 inches in length, and weighing 1.1 pounds, may be thrown by hand or projected with a heavy grenade discharger, sometimes mistakenly called a "knee mortar," The incendiary filling (white phosphorus) is contained in a brass body. An attachment consisting of a propellant and a percussion cap is screwed

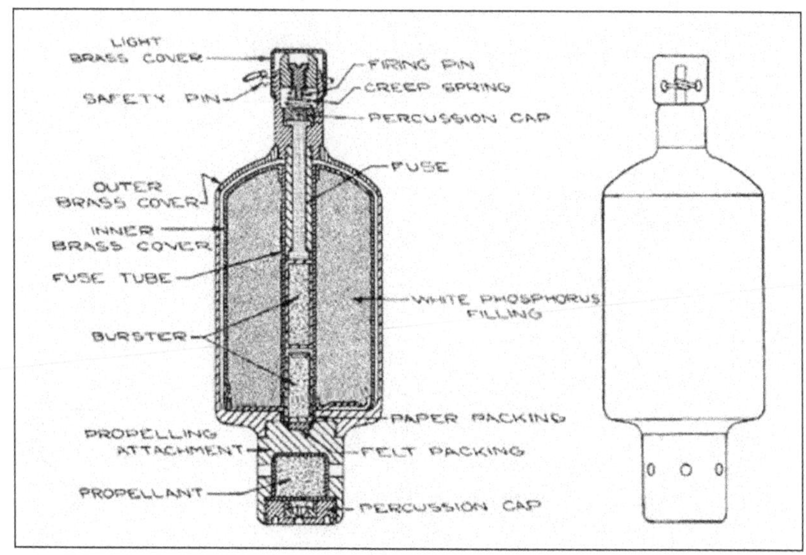

into the base of the grenade for projection with the grenade discharger. When thrown by hand, this attachment is removed. Before use, the safety pin is withdrawn. The safety pin serves the double purpose of holding a light brass cover in place and of preventing downward movement of the firing pin onto the percussion cap. The firing pin is then held off the percussion cap by a creep spring, upward movement being prevented by the light brass cover which is crimped in the middle and engages in a "V" groove cut around the ignition tube.

When used by hand, the head of the ignition tube is given a sharp tap to drive the firing pin onto the percussion cap. After a delay of 4 to 5 seconds, a fuse detonates the burster, scattering the phosphorus. When used with the grenade discharger, the shock of discharge has the same effect as tapping the grenade when thrown by hand.

B. INCENDIARY HAND GRENADE

This weapon has a diameter of 2.2 inches and an over-all length of 13.5 inches, including the wooden handle 5.3 inches in length.

The incendiary filling of the grenade is composed of white phosphorus and carbon disulfide with 41 cylindrical rubber pellets. Upon explosion, these pellets are scattered and bounce about, igniting any inflammable matter with which they may

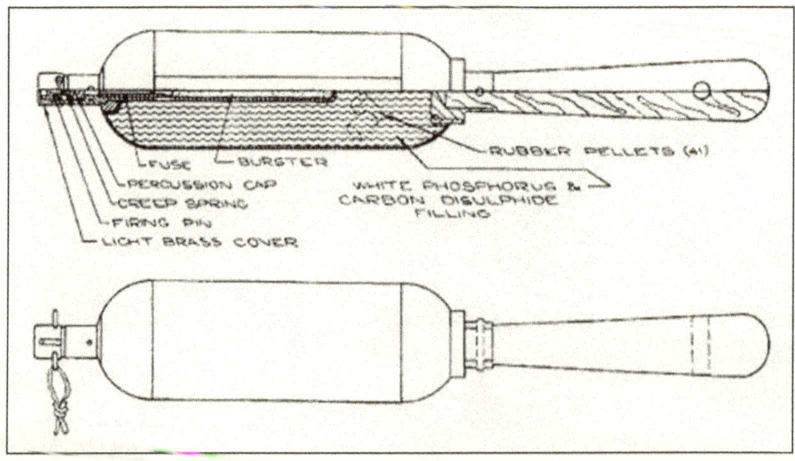

come in contact.

The detonating apparatus for this grenade is similar to that of the 1/2-kilogram incendiary grenade previously described, except that the fuse gives a delay of 6 seconds.

C. 90-MM INCENDIARY MORTAR SHELL, TYPE '94'

The incendiary filling in this bomb is similar to the hand grenade described in paragraph b above, being composed of white phosphorus and carbon disulfide with 40 cylindrical rubber pellets.

The tail arrangement is designed for one primary and six secondary charges.

The total weight of the bomb is given as 11.6 pounds, the incendiary filling as 2.2 pounds, and the burster charge as 2.8 ounces, while the over-all length is 16 inches. Its maximum range is reported to be about 4,000 yards.

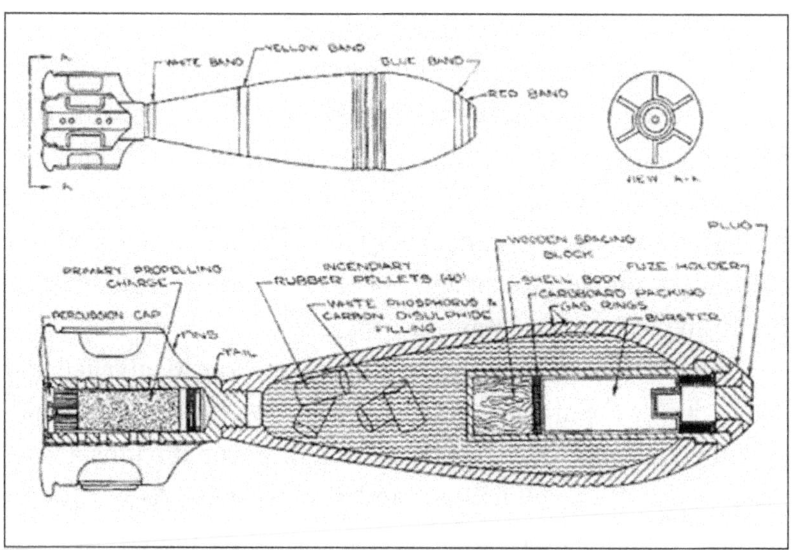

JAPANESE TACTICS IN NEW GUINEA

Tactical and Technical Trends, No. 22, April 8, 1943.

The following is a brief note on Japanese land tactics in the Milne Bay area (southeastern New Guinea). It also touches on their treatment of their own wounded.

* * * *

When the Japanese met our line of skirmishers, they fired all their machine guns into the tree-tops above our men. As soon as this fire was countered by our machine guns, their mortars opened up on our machine-gun positions.

On several occasions, when our line of skirmishers was met, large numbers of Japanese ran forward and were met by withering machine-gun fire. They immediately turned and fled. Our men, with the usual cry of "After the b******s," rushed after them with fixed bayonets. Immediately, the fleeing Japanese threw themselves on the ground and our troops ran into machine-gun fire from the Japanese rear.

In the Milne Bay area, the Japanese plan was to advance and attack during the night and then to withdraw during the daytime, leaving dozens of their men at the top of coconut palms and in the jungle, with machine guns and Tommy guns. As our forces advanced the next day, they were harassed by these remnants. Often the Japanese were tied in the tops of palm trees and remained there after they were shot. (The Japanese practice of advancing at night and hiding during the day may have been dictated on the spot by the constant strafing and reconnaissance by Allied aircraft.)

The plan eventually developed by our own forces as they advanced during the day was to drop a platoon or two each 400 or 500 yards as they advanced; eventually, they would meet the main Japanese forces. By nightfall each of the independent units and our main force would slash a perimeter clearing of about 200 yards' diameter around their positions, rig trip wires at the edge, and then confidently await the Japanese night attack. This appeared to upset the Japanese plan and proved very successful.

Considerable numbers of the Japanese wounded were evacuated by warships, but a number of cases were found of badly wounded men who apparently were considered not worth removing, having been shot through the heart by their own troops.

OPERATIONS AND TACTICS – GUADALCANAL

Tactical and Technical Trends, No. 22, April 8, 1943.

PART I: GUADALCANAL OPERATIONS

The following is an informal report on Guadalcanal operations by a high-ranking U.S. Marine officer. It is not, and was not intended to be, a complete report, but consists of observations on certain aspects only. For purposes of security certain portions of the original report have been omitted.

* * * *

LANDING OF JAPANESE REINFORCEMENTS

You are all acquainted with the endeavor of the Japanese to knock out our air and neutralize our effort on Guadalcanal. They tried it time after time without success, and their whole counteroffensive was frustrated on that account. Seeing that they could not knock the air out, they attempted on several occasions to come down with navy transports without air coverage.

Throughout late September and early October the so-called "Tokio Express" landed troops on the islands from cruisers and destroyers. This method the enemy found slow and unsatisfactory. In the first place, they could carry very few troops in the cruisers and destroyers; and in the second place, they could carry no heavy materiel. It was therefore absolutely necessary for them to come down with naval transports. On the night of the 13th and 14th of October, they came in with a striking force of surface ships off Guadalcanal. The battleships lay off Savo Island at a range of 34,500 yards. The cruisers were closer in, and the destroyers were just out of range of our 5-inch shore batteries. They bombarded Henderson Field for 2 hours and 45 minutes with 16-, 8-, and 5-inch shells. The damage to personnel was negligible. The damage to ground materiel was also negligible.

We could not prevent the convoy of six transports from coming in. One of them, however, was sunk on the way down. Four of the transports were beached in order to unload. By 1 o'clock that afternoon all four of the beached transports were on fire. The dive-bombers had accounted for three of them, and the B-17's, which flew over, accounted for one. The sixth, and remaining transport, was hit with a thousand-pound bomb. It turned away and left, together with its escort vessels. This belated destruction could not prevent the enemy from landing some 16,000 Japanese troops on the island. They did not succeed, though, in getting off very much heavy materiel. They managed to get off a company of light tanks and a battery of long-range artillery.

JAPANESE GROUND ATTACKS, OCTOBER

The Jap attacks on October 25 to 28 were ground attacks, which were a result of this landing. This was their last really major effort. It was put on by a division, plus two additional attached regiments. They attempted to cross from the west with a mass attack of tanks followed by infantry. The rivers, in the dry season (except the Lunga and the Matapona), are more in the nature of lagoons than rivers. There is a beach which closes up the mouth of the river, and they are about 15 to 20 feet deep down at the mouth. They go up to about 10 feet for 1 1/2 or 2 miles inland. There is a sand-spit that runs across the Matanika River, and the enemy (very foolishly) drove these tanks right along it. I can assure you it was certainly fine shooting for the antitank guns. They knocked out the tanks with the 37's and the 75-mm half-tracks. One enemy tank got through. It might interest you to know that he stopped over a rather deep fox-hole of a man who had the presence of mind enough to reach up with a hand grenade, place it in the tread, pull the string, and duck. It blew a tread off, and the tank wheeled around like a wounded bird, and started right out to sea. He went out until he couldn't run any further. He was then up to his turret — and so a half-track knocked that off.

The command tank in that performance, for some reason or other, decided to come straight across the river, about 50 to 60 yards up from its mouth and he was not a submarine. He just stayed there, and disappeared out of sight. Realizing that tanks don't go strolling off by themselves, we put down a concentration by 13 batteries on the west flank of the river and walked it back. The next morning we counted 657 Japanese in there.

THE NAVAL ENGAGEMENT, NOVEMBER 12

The night of November 12 was really the turning point of the whole show. The Japanese were making a major effort. They had concentrated up in Rabaul and the Shortland Islands; and also, coming down from Truk, they had from 20 to 40 merchant ships and a sizable fleet, together with 2 carriers. Their striking force for bombardment, with which they hoped to duplicate the October show, came in and was met in a very memorable battle, which almost reminded you of the days of John Paul Jones. The leading destroyer of our fleet opened up on a Japanese destroyer at 200 yards on the port bow. — The Japanese broke away.

For an hour after our ships had broken off, the Japanese were firing at each other.

The next morning, 11 transports appeared. (Our morning search-and-strike had been warned they were on the way down.) We combined a search-and-strike, and fanned out and found 11. The Southwest Pacific air arm had sunk one ship off the Shortland Islands on the way down. They had a full division, some corps troops, a full headquarters staff, and some extra regiments.

By noon, 4 of the 11 transports were sunk. By afternoon, three of the others were burning fiercely and were dead in the water. The other four were burning. The dive-bombers just ran a shuttle service from Henderson Field to the transport group, with our Grummans and P-39's acting as escort. Just as fast as they could get back and fuel and re-arm, they took off again. Those boys worked like nobody has ever worked before, to my knowledge; and certainly they did a splendid job.

That night a U.S. Navy task force came through, and much to the surprise of the Japanese it included two battleships. The opening salvo landed on a Japanese battleship, and the thing disintegrated. It was a marvelous sight to see. I had a grandstand ticket for which I paid nothing, sitting up on my observation hills, watching it. The — put another battleship out so that it could not go more than 5 knots an hour, and we sank two or three cruisers and some destroyers.

The next morning the enemy battleship was lying just north of Guadalcanal between Florida and Savo Islands, and our dive-bombers went out after it. The more they went at it, the madder they got. They hit it with 1,000-pound bombs, and our torpedo planes put their torpedoes in it. At dusk it was still there, though nobody was on it. The next morning she wasn't there.

AIR ACTION

I won't give you a day-by-day account of our air fights. We went in on the 7th, and the field was 90 percent completed. It took us 10 days to complete the strip so it could take light craft — the Grummans and the dive-bombers. A week later the P-40's and the P-39's came in. Daily, after the third day, for72 days the Japanese came down with their usual formation of 26 twin-engine high-altitude bombers. They fly a beautiful formation. They were rather inaccurate in their bombing, but I can assure you that nothing stopped them from coming for the first 10 days.

They just kept on coming, they had the air to themselves, and they came over and dropped them. When our planes got there, we were very fortunate in being able to knock down a number of Japanese planes — 541 to be exact.

Our antiaircraft consisted of 90-mm's, plus the lighter 20's, 37's, and 40's. Our antiaircraft knocked out 48 planes. I watched them one day knock out 6, and the Japanese closed in just like it was a parade formation, and kept on coming. They dropped their bombs.

As a little digression, one day after we had been bombed for about 40 days, we got word that this bomber formation was on its way down and we thought that, "Well, this is one time we up here in the jungle are not going to get hit." For there were some 12 of our merchant ships out there in the roadstead. We felt very sorry for the ships — we knew they were going to get it. However, somebody had told the Japs at Rabaul that they were to bomb Henderson Field, and they paid no more attention to those ships than if they weren't there. The bombers came right along and dropped them in the same old place on Henderson Field. This is just an idea as to how they work.

When our P-39's joined us — one squadron of them — they proved themselves to be invaluable as ground-strafing planes. We used them constantly on ground installations and they proved most valuable.

We were most fortunate towards the end to get a squadron of P-38's. They could get upstairs so fast. When we moved towards the west our air support was splendid.

I would like to say here that it is most difficult in jungle country for air reconnaissance to give you any valuable aid as to ground installations which are in dense jungle.

MAPS AND PHOTOGRAPHS

Prior to our landing, we sent our intelligence officer over to Australia. The Australians gave us what they had in the way of maps (which was practically nothing). We had one strip map that went about 500 yards inland and had been taken on a day when there were clouds around — and when you would get nice blank spaces with a picture of the clouds. We were to get additional photographs dropped on us on our way up. We got one — which did help out materially. It was of Tulagi. In that section there are practically no maps available; and, unless you do have constant aerial reconnaissance and pictures, you are going it blind. We were very fortunate on Tulagi. We met with very little resistance; and therefore the lack of maps and photographs was not such a handicap as it would have been under other conditions.

THE U.S. LANDINGS IN THE SOLOMONS

I will just give you a brief sketch of the landing. We were very fortunate on our approach day in having a very low ceiling, without a break in it. So we arrived off Savo Island without the enemy knowing we were there. At that place, the Tulagi support group went to the north of the island, and the Guadalcanal force to the south. As we approached, the opening shot was fired just off Lunga Point. A Zero float plane took off with a cold engine and flew directly at the Australia, the flag ship of the Australian cruisers. It was knocked out by broadside guns when within about 300 yards of the ship. Just at that time our dive-bombers came over and destroyed 18 float planes in the Tulagi area, and in addition destroyed 2 four-engine Japanese Navy flying boats.

The Tulagi landing was first. It was preceded by a naval gun bombardment which took the forward slopes of the hills, supported simultaneously by the dive-bombers taking the reverse slopes. It was a regimental landing, battalions in column. They landed without losing a man. They made for high ground, straddled the ridge, and turned east where the major installations of the Japanese were, throwing in a block to the west to hold whatever was there. I can assure you it was rather rough as they worked their way down through jungle country, against defenses of machine-gun nests supported by mortars.

The Japanese took to the caves and the dugouts that they had built, and tried to defend from there. We tried to drive them out of there with hand grenades, which they immediately threw back to us. When that didn't work, we tied TNT onto sticks and threw that in with a fuse. The men held them as long as they could and then threw them into the caves.

On Gavutu, which was 2 hours later, the Japanese took to the caves first but they had a good machine-gun defense of the island. We lost quite a few men there; and it goes to show that if they have enough head protection you cannot shoot them out with naval gunfire, nor can you bomb them out with aerial bombs. On Gavutu the commander, being rather air-minded, had 57 feet of rock over most of the dugouts. They were dug right into the mountains and hills.

In Guadalcanal there was not much opposition, as I said — and our air support over there, every time they had to go back to refuel, would ask for a target. We told them to drop them on Gavutu. So, in addition to getting the bombardment scheduled for it, Gavutu also got practically all of that scheduled for Guadalcanal. Yet, according to a Japanese prisoner's statement, there were only three people killed either by artillery or by ships' gunfire on that island. They were stunned, yes, but they were able to work their machine guns when the landing came off. Gavutu was pure and simple assault. The island was small. It had to be taken in a rush; and that was the way it was taken; and they were eventually driven out of their dugouts as they were driven out on Tulagi.

On Guadalcanal, the ships' guns put down a bombardment on the beach, and, as the assault boats approached the beach, the ships' guns left off. When the leading wave was within 300 yards of the beach, the aerial bombardment lifted. The scheme of maneuver there was to land regiments in column, the leading regiment to seize the beachhead which was 5 miles east of Lunga point, and the second regiment to pass through and attack — the idea being to get behind the Japanese in an endeavor to keep them from getting to the mountains. It went off as planned, with no opposition. They moved — and then the regiment which formed the beachhead moved up the beach, and another one came up the hills on the flank. That going was very dense. We arrived at Henderson Field the next morning at 10 o'clock.

The Japanese thought, according to the prisoners that we took, that it was an air-and-sea raid; and they had been instructed on Guadalcanal that in event of air-and-sea raids they were to leave the vicinity of the field, go to the jungle, and not come back until the ships left. When they came back, of course, we were there.

JAPANESE ATTACKS

The first real opposition of any kind that we met on Guadalcanal was when the Japanese Commando battalion of a thousand or twelve hundred men landed south of Henderson Field one night from two cruisers and six destroyers, and made a direct drive at the field right down the beach. Evidently their intelligence was poor or they thought very well of themselves; or perhaps there was a combination of the two. When they hit the Tenaru River, which was 15 feet deep except at the mouth, they tried to force the mouth of this river across a sand-spit in a mass rush. Our 37's loaded with cannister stopped that. We put artillery down on them and then sent a battalion down from the south and pushed them toward the sea. Then, when they were down on the beach line where it was open, we sent a company of tanks down their flank. We accounted for 670 of that Commando Group in that one location, and the next day 156 washed up from the sea.

On the night of the 14th and 15th of October, a Japanese regiment had cut their way around the field. This unit was equipped with scaling ropes every three men had one. They cut in and attacked from the south at the junction of the — Marines and the — Regiment [Army], with the — Regiment taking the brunt of the attack. There was a double-apron wire around there. The attacking battalions thought they had gotten through all the wire because their pictures did not show the other apron we had in the jungle — just on the edge of it. So, when they got through the outer apron, they rose up and with that Banzai of theirs, which they had thought would do half of the work for them, they charged. They were caught on the second apron, and 1,200 of them were knocked out with machine guns and remained at that place.

AIR SUPPORT OF LANDING OPERATIONS

I would like to give you, for what it is worth, what we who were there feel that we learned as to what is necessary for a landing force. In the first place, I don't believe that any landing against opposition is in anyway feasible unless you have an umbrella of air over you which can protect your transports, your surface ships, and your ground troops in landing. There has got to be the closest coordination and the closest timing between the bombardment of the ships' guns, and the lifting of the ships' gunfire and the picking it up by the air. For, there is a little space in there where you cannot have ships' gunfire support, because of the flat trajectory, and where your assault waves are approaching the beach — and unless somebody keeps that beach defense down, it will be rather costly.

I want to say along that line that in this instance the bombardment was beautifully coordinated by the naval air and the naval surface ships; and that from the time a battalion commander called for a concentration on a certain locality by air to the time that the concentration was delivered, it was in one instance exactly 3 1/2 minutes — which is very good going.

I would like to say a few words about the types of planes we felt should accompany a landing force in the South Pacific

Theater of Operations. Because of the type of ground we have there, and the type of islands that we have to deal with, the planes must be light aircraft capable of operating from small fields. They must be aircraft that can operate on a reasonable fuel supply.

We had some difficulties along that line. All of our fuel had to be brought in, unloaded into small boats, and then taken ashore. It was unloaded from small boats across open beach, or onto finger docks which we constructed out of palm trees and other material we had. It was then hauled to dumps, and then put into our gas carriers by hand pumps. All of that gas had to be man-handled in 50-gallon drums. The first storage tanks went into commission just about the first week in December. When we staged the B-17's through, they took a tremendous supply of gas, which we had to handle by hand in that manner. Our major labor question there was handling the gas. The sooner that you can get bulk storage into a place, the better it will be for everyone concerned.

PART II: JAPANESE OPINIONS ON AMERICAN TACTICS

These Japanese opinions on American tactics are derived from U.S. Navy sources. The Japanese based these opinions on operations in the Philippines and the fighting on Guadalcanal up to November 1942. It should be noted how strongly the Japanese emphasize the importance of infantry shock action. This is not shock action as we think of it; rather, their concept is limited to the carrying of a position with the bayonet. The emphasis is on the individual soldier, rather than the unit and the coordinated action of all arms. It will be interesting to note what changes, if any, the Japanese may make in their tactics as the result of their defeats in New Guinea and Guadalcanal.

* * * *

FOREWORD

American troops on Guadalcanal consist of a main body of Marines, whose quality in character and equipment is the pride of the American forces. With them are cooperating some Army troops and Army and Navy air forces. Although the Army forces will probably be reinforced in the future, it is estimated that the Marines will still be the backbone of their forces.

Judging by the results of the fighting up until now, the information set forth in the "Material for Study on American Tactics" just about hit the nail on the head.

The following investigates the results of their usual methods of fighting, especially in the light of past fighting on this battlefield [Guadalcanal], and will be used as a reference in the next operation.

NOTE: With regard to land warfare, this report is chiefly compiled on the basis of Army combat.

ORGANIZATION AND EQUIPMENT

The organization and equipment of the Marine force are as given in the Table of Organization and Equipment of the American Marine Division and the American Marine Force Independent Battalion, compiled by the General Staff Office in August 1942. For more on equipment and weapons, see the Army Technical Headquarters reference book.

CHARACTER (from official reports on the national characteristics of the American people).

(1) National unity is fairly strong.

(2) They like novelty and are adventurous.

(3) They are good at every sort of technique. [It is believed the Japanese mean "good in all technical matters."]

(4) Although they are given to discussion, they possess practicality. However, they take a lot of time.

(5) Although they are optimistic, they lack perseverance.

(6) The American soldier, without support of firepower, is

easily overcome and in combat is easily made to throw up his hands and surrender. If wounded, he immediately raises a cry of distress, etc. He lacks hand-to-hand fighting ability and spiritual strength. However, with the support of firepower, he acts fairly aggressively.

TRAINING

(1) Marksmanship is generally good.
(2) Hand-to-hand fighting ability is extremely poor.
(3) Night actions are inexpertly carried out.
(4) Communication technique is excellent.
(5) Reconnaissance and security patrol training is very inadequate; however, their reconnaissance aviation is generally all right.
(6) Air-ground liaison is good.
(7) The training of artillery and their method of using it are generally good.
(8) They are skillful in operating tanks and automobiles.

COMMAND AND COMBAT LEADERSHIP

(1) They subscribe to the principle that fire-power is everything, and their tactics are marked by a strong tinge of position warfare.
(2) They distribute their forces in great depth.
(3) They neglect the power of cold steel (i.e., sword and bayonet).
(4) Their flanks and rear are particularly sensitive. It is said that many times, even when only small units or patrols are on their flanks or in their rear, they have lost calmness of command [literal translation] and their actions have been hampered.

ATTACK

Even though we may say that the enemy is on the offensive, unless they have a complete faith in their material strength, especially their artillery superiority, they have a tendency not to attack. To judge by the enemy's landing on Guadalcanal and his advance to the west in the last 10 days of September, the advance of his first-line units is begun only after considerable pressure has been placed on us by ground strafing by the air force or by the fire of heavy guns. The distance they will advance at one time is limited to the range at which the main artillery force can support them from the rear. Further advance is begun after the artillery is displaced forward and preparations completed. Ordinarily the attacking forces advance during the daytime, accompanied by trench mortars and supported by artillery and aircraft. At night they generally remain at rest in the position where sunset finds them.

There is a tendency for the main body to keep close to both sides of roads and not utilize the jungle, except for small forces and patrols. If they stop and do not move out for a day or two, they construct light wire entanglements.

DEFENSIVE FIGHTING

Although they make it a principle to destroy the enemy in front of the main line of resistance of a defensive position, they also advocate active counterattacks within the positions. [The Japanese principle of defense is to give with the blow, let the attacking enemy become disorganized by his advance, and then counterattack in force.]

In front of and within their positions, they prepare thorough concentrations of firepower, especially that of trench mortars and artillery, and they use ammunition abundantly. Furthermore, in not a few cases, the troops holding the position fell back and then artillery fire was concentrated in the area they had evacuated. Also, artillery fire concentrations are laid down in the jungle in front of the positions. There are units that have received heavy casualties on this account. It seems that they carry out test firing beforehand at each place. [This must mean registration fire. It is amazing to find a remark like this. It shows a remarkable lack of appreciation, on the part of the Japanese, of the capabilities and limitations of artillery. This has been intimated by other sources.]

They install microphones in front of and within positions, and utilize mobile artillery-observation stations to perceive our approach so that fire may be concentrated on our force. The "mikes" are gray in color and of large type, in large leather cases. They are installed at the roots of trees, etc. The wires are black insulated wire.

Their airplanes, particularly fighters, reconnoiter and make bombing and strafing attacks, and act very aggressively. As the fighters carry out their strafing and bombing at low altitudes by diving, there are frequent opportunities to shoot them down when infantry units can carry out AA firing.

Their forward units sometimes use a successive resistance. [Probably means delaying actions.]

For security to the front of their positions, they send out forces about the size of a platoon and generally avoid posting sentries in small groups, with the result that there are many gaps. The security measures in the position itself are also insufficient, and it often happens during a battle that our patrols stumble upon enemy positions and find AA gun positions, provisions, dumps, etc. On account of their not posting observers in front of the positions, the attackers [i.e., Japanese] sometimes, contrary to what might be expected, suddenly and without warning come in contact with the main position and receive unexpected losses.

Although their counterattacks are not vigorous, they sometimes execute them against our flanks and rear at very short distances in front of their positions. However, they don't use cold steel (bayonets).

NATURE OF DEFENSIVE POSITIONS

Their wire entanglements consist of roof-shaped and net-shaped entanglements, and low wire entanglements, and are constructed over the whole front of the position. Although there are three or four bands of wire at important points, there are also light entanglements of about three strands of barbed wire. Empty cans and so forth are fastened to the wires. Electrically charged wire entanglements have not yet been observed.

Pillboxes are chiefly covered machine-gun positions, and are deployed in depth every 200 or 300 yards along the front. Many log ones have been used, but as yet none of the concrete type have been observed for certain.

At present the enemy is burning back the jungle here and there to clear the field of fire, establishing more covered machine-gun positions, and constructing other installations so the positions will be made increasingly stronger.

WITHDRAWAL TACTICS

Withdrawal from the field is carried out under the protection of the main artillery force. When in a coastal area, they use landing boats a great deal.

NIGHT FIGHTING

They fire actively at night, especially trench mortars, and where preparation has been made, the fire has considerable effect. They almost never make night attacks.

PATROLLING

Extremely few patrols are sent out, and when they execute a reconnaissance mission, it is generally with a platoon or a larger force, and almost like a reconnaissance in force. The afternoon of September 24, about 100 of the enemy appeared in the vicinity of the OKA Force's observation post and ran into some of our people who were cooking. They were scouting in preparation for the advance which the enemy made several days later in the vicinity of the Matanika River.

They carry out vigorous air reconnaissance. They execute especially thorough strafing and bombing attacks when they spot the smoke of our cooking fires, or when our soldiers are moving in the open.

MISCELLANEOUS

Their tanks traverse almost any kind of terrain; however, their action is independent, and there should be many opportunities to take advantage of this.

Automobiles are used everywhere in large numbers, and are used even off the roads.

POINTS TO NOTE IN OUR COMBAT

(1) In many cases our attacks on positions are ineffective without organized fire support. Even a night attack must have a thorough artillery preparation, and we should not hesitate to use firepower support forces. [The composition of these "firepower support forces" is probably battalion and regimental infantry guns, 37-mm antitank guns, mortars, and machine guns: in other words, the infantry heavy weapons. The Japanese have a tendency to neglect proper use of these, placing their dependence on the maneuver and "cold steel."]

(2) In infantry fighting at close quarters, crawling forward and utilizing dead ground has many advantages.

(3) The terrain of the battlefield is generally hilly; on high ground are mostly grassy plains, and in the low places there is jungle. In the jungle we can conceal our intentions, but it is extremely difficult to maintain direction there, so it is necessary to make careful plans and preparations beforehand, and to gain and maintain complete control of the unit.

(4) It is difficult to determine (in the jungle) where one is and where the objective of the attack is; therefore, it is necessary for commanding officers of all units to have a complete knowledge of the locality, the route of attack, etc.

(5) Effective shelling is often received in the jungle in front of the enemy positions, and there have been cases where

this disorganized the ranks and ultimately rendered a charge impossible. The commanding officer must give special attention to the control of his force.

(6) Search out the "mike" positions, and at a predesignated time destroy them simultaneously, taking care to cut the wires.

(7) Since the enemy reacts very quickly to our artillery fire, we should establish artillery positions everywhere, and by utilizing dummy positions, smoke, etc., confuse the enemy and make him waste his shells. In not a few cases, the skillful establishment of false positions at the front and flanks of important points occupied by the infantry in the face of the enemy has been attended with great success.

(8) While preparing the attack, full attention should be given to the supply and concentration of ammunition, provisions, water, and so forth.

(9) If we close with their firepower [Translator's note: This phrase may also be translated "closely allied with firepower."], our cold steel still has a decisive force and the enemy fears it greatly.

(10) Considering the difficulties of the terrain, unusual amounts of exertion and time must be expended in the preparation for the attack.

(11) As the health situation is not good, the men must not be allowed to catch cold while they sleep.

(12) In case you stay rather long in one place, air-raid trenches must be dug, without fail. If the earthworks are completed, any sort of concentrated fire, or bombing, can be withstood without great loss.

(13) During the day, smoke from cooking fires is absolutely forbidden. In case of cooking at night, you must not allow firelight to show.

CONCLUSION

To sum up, the enemy's military preparations may be said to be built on a framework of a materialistically organized firepower, with the benefits of air activity added. They are never seen to maintain any particular fighting power, and although they are at present exerting themselves in the extreme and strengthening their positions, if we make especially thorough preparations, prepare our fighting strength to deal hammerlike blows against the enemy, concentrate on using all sorts of original plans, and carry them out with a flourishing aggressive spirit, our success in the present operation is certainly beyond doubt.

FIGHTING ON THE KOKODA TRAIL IN NEW GUINEA

Tactical and Technical Trends, No. 23, April 22, 1943.

Direct reports from the front are always worth reading. Even if there is some repetition of detail, the repetition itself drives home important lessons. The notes that follow were sent in by a U.S. Army Colonel.

* * * *

In the fighting on the Kokoda Trail, (between Port Moresby and Buna) our troops found that on making contact along a road or trail in the jungle, the Japanese usually followed this procedure:

An especially trained advance guard pushed ahead of their column, took up a position astride the trail, and tried to pin down our defense with machine-gun and mortar fire. Next, if various feints and demonstrations did not induce us to give away our position by opening a premature fire, the Japs would try to infiltrate around the flanks. Their groups moved swiftly under cover; targets were poor and fleeting. If our troops held their fire till a good target presented itself, these forward groups could usually be stopped. There were many cases where, when the advance elements were allowed to sneak by, the supports which followed them could be ripped up by machine-gun and rifle fire. However, if the defense disclosed its position by too early or too powerful a fire, the Japanese brought up machine guns and mortars and blasted our lines.

To test the possibility of further advance, the Japanese used many tricks based on two natural human traits - fear of the unseen and unknown, and curiosity. They appeared to place much confidence in the effect of noise, and for this reason did considerable firing, both to bolster their own courage and to lower our morale. Captured weapons were shot off to give the impression that our men were firing them; they fired machine guns out on the flank to give the impression that our position was being turned; or they talked loudly and shook bushes to draw nervous shots or cause movement. In order to distract attention and cause confusion, they exploded fire-crackers.

There must be depth to positions in order to prevent effective encirclement, and bold handling of combat patrols to meet their flanking tactics. The counterattack cannot be overstressed. All-around defense, at night, or in thick country, is necessary.

In their attack on prepared positions, the Japanese used a more or less standard procedure. By reconnaissance and ruses, they made every effort to determine our strength and location. After they had discovered what they thought was a soft spot, they persisted in attacking there. Should the first attack fail, it was shifted to some other place, but the Japanese usually returned again to the original point of attack. Consequently, it was dangerous to weaken that point to reinforce some other.

Often, in this phase of the fighting, the Japanese used no preparatory fire. After contact was made, their skirmish line hit the ground while overhead fire by machine guns and mortars fell on our positions. Under cover of the barrage, supports would try to crawl close enough to put down a hand-grenade barrage to protect the advance. It was not uncommon during such attacks for the enemy to replace tired forward troops with fresh reserves. This change-over was accomplished efficiently, and without confusion.[5] Incidentally, the Japanese will advance under a white flag and shoot at anyone coming out, disguise himself as a native or a civilian, and in retreat, litter the trail with cast-off garments and equipment to give the impression of a disorderly flight, and then ambush the pursuit.

5 The description of these skirmish line tactics corresponds closely with accounts of Indian fighting in Kentucky and Ohio in Daniel Boone's day.

SOME JAPANESE DEFENSIVE METHODS

Tactical and Technical Trends, No. 24, May 6, 1943.

In previous issues of Tactical and Technical Trends, references have been made to some defensive tactics used by the Japanese. The following notes from British sources give added emphasis to this subject and are reported here in order to facilitate recognition of these tactics.

A. GENERAL

Japanese tactical methods in the defense conform basically to normal practice, but they are characterized by a very high standard of camouflage. Except in marshy country, where the Japanese build up to as much as 8 feet above ground level, it is difficult to spot their positions, which are skillfully hidden under bushes, hedges, and buildings and even under the roots of big trees. Whether in jungle or other country, the principle of all-around defense is strictly applied, and positions have so far presented no weak spots. Defended areas, however small, are self-contained with regard to ammunition and food, and they are stubbornly defended—literally to the last man. Japanese seriously wounded have been found still grasping hand grenades which they have been too weak to throw, and on other occasions repeated offers of quarter in a hopeless situation have been refused.

The information given below is based on experiences in New Guinea and the Solomons, and while principles—such as depth in the defense, all-around defense, and the application of camouflage—do not alter, details such as the employment of supporting weapons and the construction of defenses, will vary considerably according to the nature of the country. This point should be remembered when studying what the Japanese have done in the dense jungle of New Guinea, so as to be prepared for something different in the more open spaces of, say, Central Burma and China.

B. ORGANIZATION OF DEFENSIVE POSITION

The Japanese choose positions on commanding ground and site their defended areas in great depth along the line of communication.

Weapons are sited to cover all approaches and are protected by booby traps. Weapon pits are small and cleverly concealed. They normally contain one or two men and are often linked by tunnels. Whether in swampy or dry ground, overhead cover is often constructed.

Automatic weapons are sited to fire along prepared lines which intersect. These lines are cut in the jungle to a height of about 2 feet, presenting a tunnel effect. 30-caliber heavy MGs are likely to be sited well forward and sub-allotted to platoon localities. Positions containing automatic weapons are frequently protected by snipers in trees near the position. Men in trees have also been reported on the flanks of positions.

In swampy areas, two types of earthworks are constructed. The first, called in the Southwest Pacific the "bunker" type, consists of a trench with closely timbered sides and top. The trench is covered by a mound which is built up with coconut-log piles laid lengthwise and packed with earth. The height of the mound and the depth of the trench vary according to the level of the swamp water. Some mounds rise to about 8 feet above ground level. These mounds have slits at ground level for automatic weapons, and the positions are connected by crawl trenches. The mounds give protection to the defenders against mortar and antipersonnel bombs and limit the effect of 25-pounder (88-mm) shells. Positions are camouflaged with local natural materials.

The second type of earthwork is similar in appearance to the first, but it is constructed without loopholes and used for concealment and protection from artillery and mortar fire. Attacking troops, attracted by these raised earthworks, tend to make them their objectives and are then caught in the fire from posts constructed at ground level on the flanks and in rear of these earthworks.

In addition to the construction of these earthworks, the Japanese pay particular attention to the careful digging of dugouts. In the Solomon Islands, for instance, it was found that hand grenades could be thrown into Japanese dugouts but, owing to the special construction of the entrance, they exploded harmlessly inside without killing the occupants, who were subsequently able to emerge and fire into the rear of our troops. In this area the dugouts were cut back into a hillside and were sited so as to be mutually supporting. They were constructed to hold about eight men each and were faced on the front and flanks with sand bags and steel plates. Their layout was as shown in the diagram (see Tactical and Technical Trends, No. 10, p. 13). Telephone cables are laid between defended localities, but according to information received so far, visual methods of intercommunication, such as flag or shutter, have not been employed.

C. CONDUCT OF DEFENSE

In jungle country the fire fight takes place at ranges of between 50 and 100 yards. It has been found especially necessary to make a short pause between igniting the fuze of a grenade and throwing it, as otherwise the Japanese are adept at throwing them back. The Japanese make frequent use of small local counterattacks conducted by 8 or 10 men and led by an officer.

D. DECEPTIVE TACTICS; NEW GUINEA

The following notes summarize some of the tactics used by the Japanese in the New Guinea area. The extensive use again made of deceptive tactics should be noted.

(1) When the Japanese met the enemy line of skirmishers they fired all their machine guns into the tree-tops above their opponents. As soon as this fire was countered by Allied machine guns, the Japanese mortars opened up on these machine-gun positions.

(2) On several occasions when the Allied line of skirmishers was met, large numbers of Japanese ran forward and were met by a withering machine-gun fire. They immediately turned round and fled. Allied troops with the usual cry of "After the bastards" immediately rushed forward with fixed bayonets. Immediately, the fleeing Japanese threw themselves on the ground and Allied soldiers ran into machine-gun fire from the Japanese rear.

(3) In the Milne Bay area the Japanese plan was to advance and attack during the night and then to withdraw during the daytime, leaving dozens of their men in the tops of coconut palms, and in the jungle, with automatic weapons. As Allied forces advanced the next day, they were harassed by these remnants. Often the Japanese were tied in the tops of the palm trees and remained there after they were shot.

(4) There were times when it was felt that the Japanese troops might have surrendered, but in no case did they do so. It was a question of keeping at them until every man was killed.

(5) Counter Tactics

The plan eventually developed by Allied forces, as they advanced during the day, was to drop a platoon or two each 4 to 5 hundred yards apart as they advanced, and eventually they would meet the main Japanese forces. By nightfall each of the independent posts and the main force would slash a perimeter clearing of about 200 yards diameter around their posts, rig trip wires at the edge, and then confidently await the Japanese night attack. This appeared to upset the Japanese plan and proved very successful.

FURTHER NOTES ON THE MALAYAN CAMPAIGN

Tactical and Technical Trends, No. 24, May 6, 1943.

To some extent there may be an element of repetition in the report which follows, but even granting that such is the case, this will serve to highlight the lessons derived from actual experience.

"We must know our foes and know them well," writes the American compiler of the following notes, which indicate some of the basic tactics used by the Japanese in the Malayan Campaign.

"On the tactical side the campaign was an excellent example of 'jungle warfare' and of the use of waterways as arteries of communication and movement. Throughout the campaign there was none, or practically none, of the fanatic frontal charges which characterized Jap tactics in North China. In Malaya it was a case of constant infiltration and constant small-scale envelopment.

"Many of the envelopments were over water and involved landing behind the Allied front. In these 'water-land' operations the experience gained along the Yangtze River and elsewhere in China no doubt was of real value, but most of the Malayan landings had a character uniquely their own. In China the landings habitually were made under the guns of the Navy. The same was true of the basic landing at Kota Bahru, where half-a-dozen Jap troop transports stood off-shore while the troops reached the beaches in various types of special landing crafts.

"But most of the tactical landings involved in the envelopments under discussion occurred on the western coast where, of course, there was no Jap naval support. These landings generally were small in size—perhaps a company or two, or at the most a battalion. The Japs made great use of what they found locally in the way of floating craft, and in view of the size of the Malayan fishing fleet what they found was considerable. In addition, there is evidence that a few special landing craft, motorized and with a capacity for as many as 100 men each, were transported overland from Singora for use along the western coast.

"A characteristic of the Japanese landings was the evident use of alternative objectives. There are several instances in which a convoy, encountering resistance at one point on the coast, moved up or down coast to another more favorable point. Thus was the principle of infiltration applied to tactical landings.

"Infiltration or jungle warfare are the words generally applied to the actual fighting off the roads as it occurred throughout Malaya. The basic Jap tactic involved extreme decentralization: giving a small unit or even an individual soldier an objective, and telling it or him to get there. In the process of getting there the Jap practice was constantly to seek to slip through or, if attack was necessary, to make it from a flank. All accounts agree on the reluctance of the Japs to push ahead frontally."

PROTECTION OF JAP TANKS AGAINST STICKY GRENADES

Tactical and Technical Trends, No. 25, May 20, 1943.

Two Japanese tanks captured in the Solomon Islands were coated all over with grease, apparently to prevent sticky grenades from adhering.

SOME BRITISH OBSERVATIONS OF JAPANESE TACTICS

Tactical and Technical Trends, No. 26, June 3, 1943.

From a very recent British report, the following observations on Japanese tactics have been selected. Quite possibly, some or many of the details are already known to our troops, but there appears to be much of general interest in these notes. It is worthy of mention that the British are making use of our experience as we are of theirs.

* * * *

A. A HINT ABOUT PASS WORDS

The old Japanese trick of using the language of our troops to try and discover our positions has again been used in Burma.

One voice was heard shouting in Bengali "Don't shoot, we are the -- Rifles. Where are you?" On other occasions English and Urdu (a Hindu language) were used.

It is, however, generally quite simple to distinguish whether friend or foe is calling, as the Japanese find many of our words impossible to pronounce correctly.

The following short table indicates the manner in which the Japanese would pronounce certain groupings of English letters. Note that they substitute "r" for "l," "su" or "za" for "th," and "b" for "v."

Words employing any two or all of the letters would certainly be mispronounced by Japanese. It is useful to bear this in mind when formulating pass words.

English Letters	Japanese Phonetic Pronunciation
La	Rah (soft r)
Ly	Rye (soft r)
Th	Su (soft s as in "soft")
The	Za or Zeh
Very	Bedy (y like double "e" in "see")
Velvet	Berubet

B. RECONNAISSANCE METHODS

A number of Japanese documents from fighting areas show how the Japanese stress the importance of reconnaissance.

Scouts are instructed to sketch hostile dispositions from observation posts and to bring back their reports without taking any unnecessary risks. Urgent reports, it is stated, must be made by telephone or orally and afterwards confirmed by sketch maps. In reconnaissance much use is made of all available natives.

In New Guinea the primary task of reconnaissance was the pinpointing of positions: personal reconnaissance by officer patrols took place. Preparations for night attacks in Guadalcanal included the sending out of scouts "since enemy security during the night is not always sufficient." Officers were ordered to "study aerial photographs and reconnaissance reports in detail, remembering outstanding features in the area to be attacked."

C. APPROACH THROUGH JUNGLE

The following extracts from a divisional order secured in Guadalcanal illustrate the detailed precautions taken by the Japanese when approaching a combat area.

"Even though the march through dense forest at night is planned beforehand, there are naturally many occasions when maintenance of contact is difficult. For this reason, during movement at night lights should be used. It may be necessary to use glow worms taken from dead trees to maintain contact.

"If one man is ordered to carry out the work of cutting away the undergrowth through the dense forest, the march will be impossible. A squad of 30 men and an officer is necessary as a clearing squad under jungle conditions to keep the column moving.

"Contact in the forest must be maintained by the use of a small whistle, and it is very important not to shout. The enemy often sets up a microphone on elevated ground and directs his artillery fire when our position is known."

D. CAMOUFLAGE

In certain instances, gun emplacements have been camouflaged by building up the sides of a gradual slope and coloring the whole position to correspond with the sand or soil surrounding it. The tone blending is complete, but the circular outline remains clearly visible. Overhead covering is not used on this type. In other types, overhead covers are used, the cover being a "flat" made up of a net interlaced with cut scrub. The position is none the less easily observed because of signs of activity on the trails and the tendency of the Japanese to cover only the area immediately over the gun. They also neglect to bridge the "slashed" area in the virgin scrub, which surrounds the emplacement.

In one area our troops found four well-camouflaged guns. Here, a net interlaced with garlands and strewn with small bushes to give relief was used to hide the guns. However, they were readily discernible on photographs because the camouflage did not form a complete cover. The ground surface could be seen, and the light sand, where the emplacement had been dug, revealed its position.

Dazzle painting is another form of camouflage used. The general procedure has been to paint the roof and sides with wavy zebra-like stripes of alternate light and dark colors. Usually, bands of dark and light stripes continue from the eaves, but some roofs are painted with a band of light and dark stripes up to the ridge, and with the contrasting colors from the ridge down to the opposite gutter. This latter method forms a distinct line of demarcation along the ridge of the roof and destroys the illusion. These bands do not average more than 10 feet wide; regardless of the length of the building. Another type of dazzle painting is to paint the roof and sides with spots of dark color on a light background, in a manner that can best be compared to the spots on a giraffe.

The Japanese have been relatively successful in hiding some objects by completely covering them with earth. They have guarded against detection by building a slope of low gradient, thereby achieving the minimum relief.

E. DEFENSIVE BUNKERS

(1) General Remarks

The Japanese are evidently exponents of the theory that the construction of a defensive position involves a continual process of development. It is normal for a new defensive position first to take the form of a series of fox-holes, which are subsequently, if time and circumstances permit, linked together into a coordinated defense system. Such a position may well include still other fox-holes, which are difficult both to locate and to eliminate. The third stage of development takes the form of the construction of strongpoints, or "bunker" type earthworks as they have been called in New Guinea. These strongpoints, as seen in Burma, fall into two types, both of which are illustrated in the accompanying sketch.

(2) The Double-Bay Bunker

These are built in two sizes, 25 ft. by 15 ft., and 60 ft. by 40 ft. They consist of mounds of earth from 5 ft. to 12 ft. in height, with a rear entrance well recessed into the mound. Forward, a central, apparently solid, block projects to form two bays. These bays vary in size. The smaller-size earthworks form part of the main trench system, with which they are linked, but the large "bunkers" appear to be isolated.

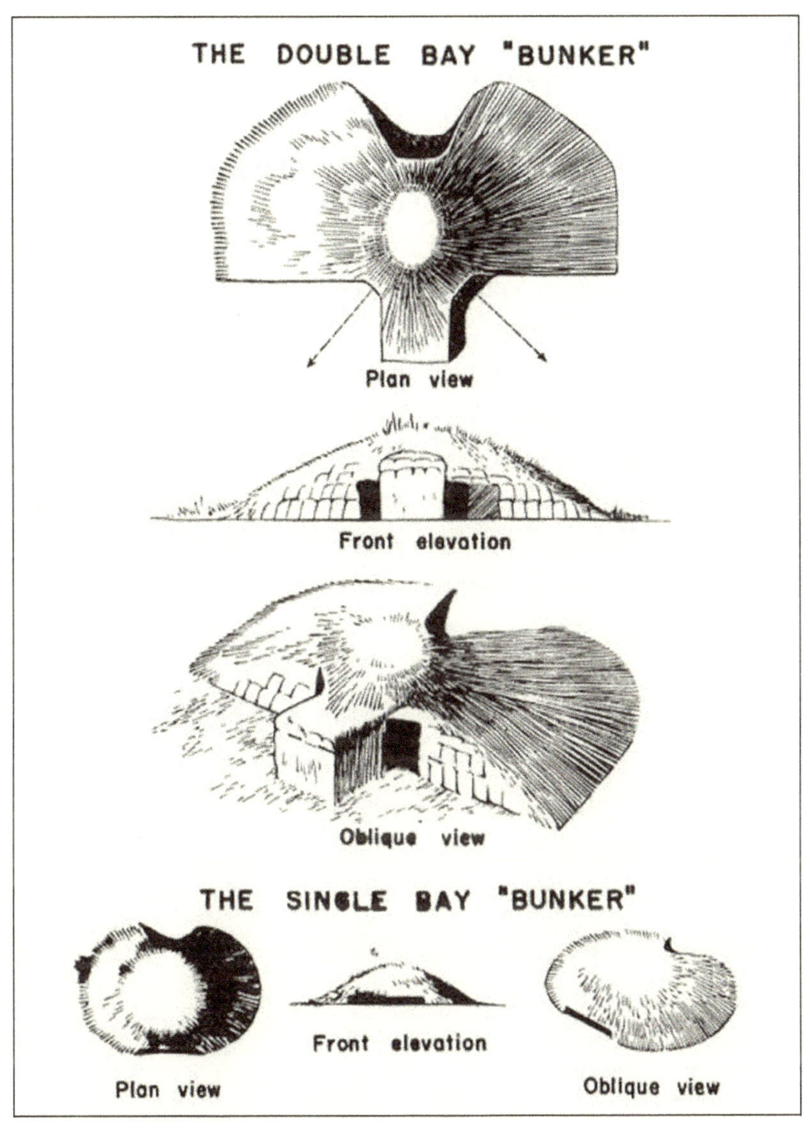

(3) The Single-Bay Bunker

This consists of a roughly circular mound of earth about 25 ft. in diameter and 5 ft. high, with entrance at the rear, opening on to a crawl trench or the main trench system. In front is a firing-slit at, or slightly above, ground level, from 6 to 8 ft. long and about 1 1/2 to 2 ft. high. Inside there is presumably a timbered dugout partly below ground level.

Comment: Up to now these bunker strongpoints have been identified in Burma in beach defense positions only, though there seems no reason to think that they cannot be equally well employed elsewhere should any particular position warrant such a comparatively elaborate defense.

It appears that these defensive positions are normally occupied in the first instance by a platoon armed with their usual weapons--light machine guns, rifles, and grenade dischargers. A position covering a front of some 600 yards may seem a very large assignment for one platoon, but this wide dispersion seems to be standard Japanese practice in the defense.

In the later stages of development of a position, when the strongpoints have been constructed, the platoon is probably strengthened by detachments from the machine-gun company or battalion infantry gun platoon. They appear to use both the single- and double-bay bunkers as positions for their heavy machine guns. The double-bay type may also be used as covered emplacements for their antitank guns. This does not preclude the use of either type also as positions for the normal automatic weapons of the platoon.

JAPANESE TACTICS IN THE MILNE BAY OPERATIONS

Tactical and Technical Trends, No. 26, June 3, 1943.

A. GENERAL

The present tactics and techniques of the Japanese have been developed as the result of combat experience against active enemies under varied conditions and over many types of terrain.

As is generally known now, the Japanese are cunning fighters, skilled in the use of ruse and deception. They are well trained in the tactics of infiltration, especially in jungle and mountain country. Their favorite maneuver is the turning of an exposed flank. During the entire Milne Bay operation (see Tactical and Technical Trends, p. 28, No. 22 for previous reference to this operation), Allied flanks were never secure, because the Japanese had practically complete immunity by sea and so could make landings at any chosen point.

While it is true that the tactics employed at Milne Bay should be regarded as applicable to a particular terrain rather than as representing the normal situation in jungle warfare, yet the principles illustrated and the lessons learned are of general application.

B. PATROLS

(1) Strength

From Japanese sources it is learned that in this operation the patrol strength for special tasks was one officer and six enlisted men, or one non-commissioned officer and three enlisted men. Normal night patrols numbered 18 men or more, while day patrols averaged from 6 to 10 men. In general, these patrols moved as a body and kept to the trails. Combat patrols were not employed by the Japanese for reconnaissance.

(2) Employment

Scouts made use of the thick jungle to approach our defense areas, or were left in position when the enemy withdrew from a night attack. In general, they would lie "doggo" and unobserved in order to get information to their troops. They allowed our patrols and working parties to pass unmolested.

c. Night Operations

The Japanese force relied almost entirely on night operations, for which it appeared to have been well trained.

There were no Japanese attacks by day and movement was limited. This might have been due to our complete command of the air. The main Japanese body rested by day with little regard for local security.

d. Approach March

During the approach march, the Japanese moved rapidly, in groups of 20 to 30, with little regard to flank protection. The main line of advance was the road or beach. Bodies of troops did not seem to have moved more than 300 yards from the road. A speed of movement was achieved which would have been impossible if an attempt was made to secure the flanks. Enemy troops talked a good deal during the approach march, but were careful about lights. Absolute silence was maintained just before the attack and while assembling.

e. Night attacks

During the assembly for the attack, Japanese troops tended to bunch up. Once the attack began, they made all the noise possible by firing mortars, grenades, and fire crackers, and by calling and whistling. This noise was made not only to draw our fire but also in an attempt to demoralize our troops and to encourage their own.

Night attacks were made on a small frontage, but mortars were fired well forward to the flanks to give an impression of a large force advancing on a wide front. The rear elements seemed to be more widely deployed for a probable flank envelopment.

When our troops opened fire, the Japanese tried to infiltrate through our flanks and rear. When in position, they attempted to rush our posts under cover of mortar fire and grenades.

f. Night Withdrawals

These night attacks were suddenly broken off before daylight. The Japanese withdrew again in chattering groups along the road. In two instances, the signal to withdraw was a bugle call. Snipers and observers in trees close to our main line of resistance and along trails were left behind as they withdrew. A great deal of equipment was abandoned, but no wounded were left.

g. Sniping and Field Craft

The Japanese used tree snipers to harass our troops during the day and interfere with the advance. Before opening fire the snipers would allow our troops to approach within a few yards, or to go past. These snipers cooperated with others hidden on the ground. When our troops exposed themselves to shoot at tree snipers, they drew fire from the ground. Other snipers lay hidden among their own dead and allowed our patrols and burial parties to go past before firing. The snipers' marksmanship was not as good as their fieldcraft.

The fieldcraft of these snipers was very good. They used foliage and body camouflage nets and secured themselves in the leafy tops of coconut palms and other trees. Their greenish uniform blended well with the vegetation. They were so well hidden that it was necessary to draw their fire in order to discover their position. Even then they were difficult to dislodge.

h. Defense

Japanese tactics in this action were mainly centered on attack. All defense positions were covered by a screen of snipers who were hard to deal with.

i. Infantry Cooperation with Tanks

At least two light tanks were used by the Japanese in this operation. Some machine gunners rode on the tanks or followed close behind. The glare of the headlamps prevented our troops from seeing these troops. In defiles, other infantry parties preceded the tanks to deal with antitank guns lying in ambush.

j. Deception

In addition to skillful fieldcraft, the Japanese made free use of English phrases in ruses to draw fire. Some were well chosen to give the impression that bodies of our troops were approaching the position; examples were "Do not fire, troops coming in," etc. However, a few of these expressions were quite inappropriate—as "Good morning" in the middle of the night, etc.

k. Recommendations by Brigade Commanders

(1) Communications

Jungle fighting presents great difficulties for signal communication. Visual signaling is often impossible. To counteract this situation, it was recommended that a large and immediate reserve of wire and spare telephones be made available for issue to battalions in this type of operation. In all cases where lines and telephones were available, signal communication was maintained in the heaviest undergrowth.

(2) Transport

Only vehicles with high clearance and 4-wheel drives are recommended for this type of operation; also, that each company (if possible each platoon) be equipped with a light 2-wheel cart similar to the type captured from the Japanese. These carts are invaluable for rapid transport of mortar bombs, supplies, and ammunition, and in some cases for the evacuation of the wounded.

(3) Clothing

Recommendation was made that all enlisted men be issued

capes equipped with cross-straps in place of the present type, which is a sort of cape thrown over the shoulders with a series of buttons down the front. It is awkward to handle, especially if the soldier is called upon to use his rifle.

(4) Ordnance

In place of drum magazines for Thompson submachine guns, it was proposed that the box type magazine be carried. Bayonets should be sharpened to a cutting edge to assist in the quick clearance of undergrowth. It was recommended that Royal Australian Air Force type signal pistols and cartridges be issued, so that a more economical signal ammunition code would be established for the recognition of troops in forward areas, instead of the method involving considerable expenditure of Very cartridges. Finally, it was recommended that guns place one round of smoke on each side of the target to indicate positions to aircraft for bombing and strafing. This method was tried, and the round of smoke was placed on each side of the target according to the direction of the wind. This proved very effective, as the smoke drifted very slowly, hung about the tops of the trees, and was easily sighted by Allied planes.

ABOUT CODA BOOKS

Most Coda books are edited and endorsed by Emmy Award winning film maker and military historian Bob Carruthers, producer of Discovery Channel's Line of Fire and Weapons of War and BBC's Both Sides of the Line. Long experience and strong editorial control gives the military history enthusiast the ability to buy with confidence.

The series advisor is David McWhinnie, producer of the acclaimed Battlefield series for Discovery Channel. David and Bob have co-produced books and films with a wide variety of the UK's leading historians including Professor John Erickson and Dr David Chandler.

Where possible the books draw on rare primary sources to give the military enthusiast new insights into a fascinating subject.

www.codabooks.com

The English Civil Wars

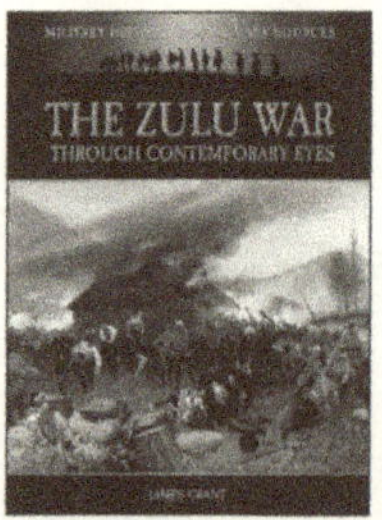

The Zulu Wars

Into Battle with Napoleon 1812

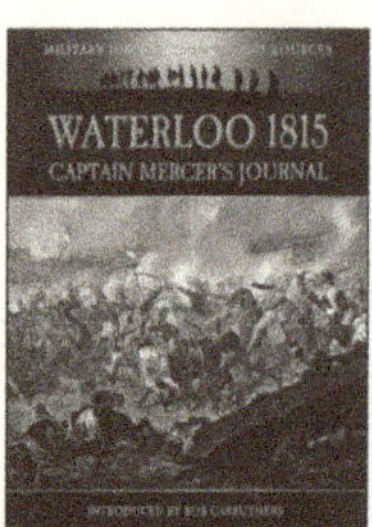

Waterloo 1815

The Anglo-Saxon Chronicle

The Battle of the Bulge

The Normandy Campaign 1944

Hitler's Justification for WWII

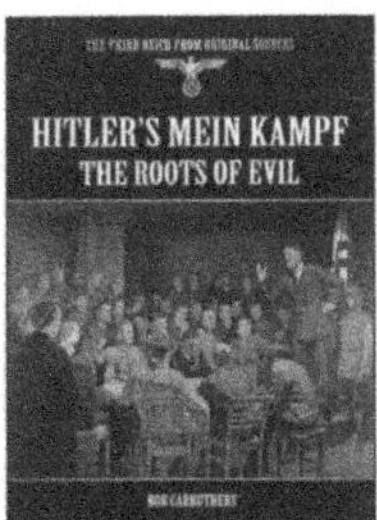

Hitler's Mein Kampf - The Roots of Evil

I Knew Hitler

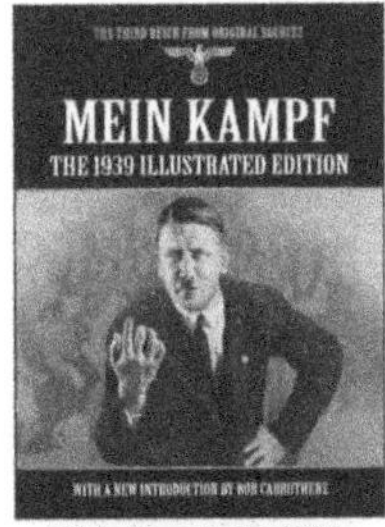

Mein Kampf - The 1939 Illustrated Edition

The Nuremberg Trials Volume 1

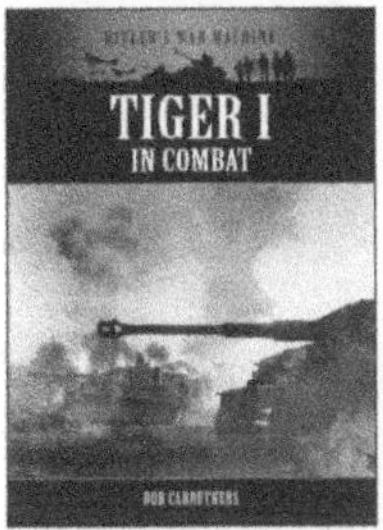

Tiger I in Combat

Tiger I Crew Manual

Panzers at War 1939-1942

Panzers at War 1943-1945

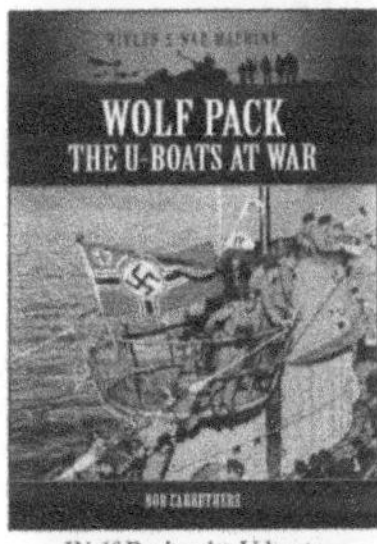

Wolf Pack - the U boats

Poland 1939

Luftwaffe Combat Reports

Eastern Front Night Combat

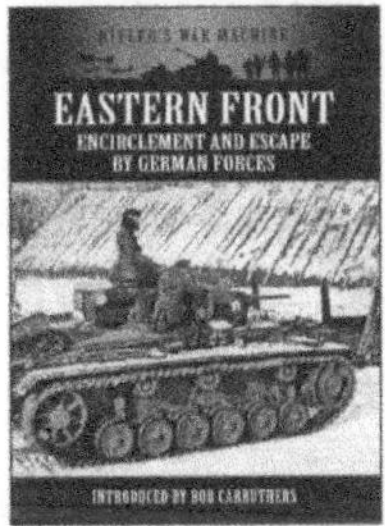

Eastern Front Encirclement

Panzer Combat Reports

The Panther V in Combat

The Red Army in Combat

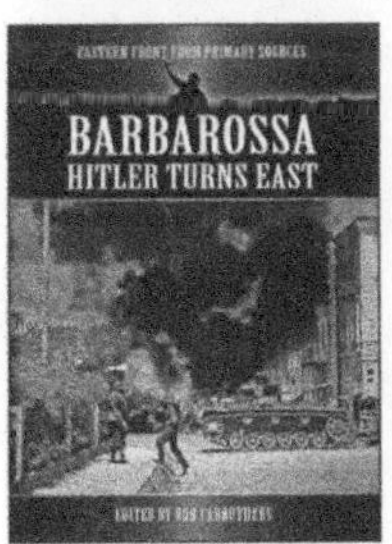

Barbarossa - Hitler Turns East

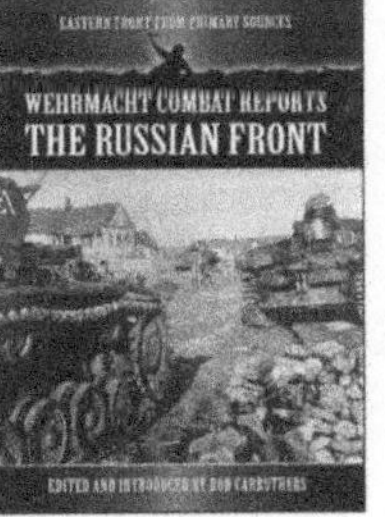

The Russian Front

The Wehrmacht in Russia

Servants of Evil

www.ingramcontent.com/pod-product-compliance
Lightning Source LLC
Chambersburg PA
CBHW021147090426
42740CB00008B/977

* 9 7 8 1 7 8 1 5 8 3 2 4 1 *